A Companion Guide
to Handbook of Urban
Educational Leadership

A Companion Guide to Handbook of Urban Educational Leadership

Theory to Practice

Edited by
René O. Guillaume
Noelle Witherspoon Arnold
Azadeh F. Osanloo

ROWMAN & LITTLEFIELD
Lanham • Boulder • New York • London

Published by Rowman & Littlefield
An imprint of The Rowman & Littlefield Publishing Group, Inc.
4501 Forbes Boulevard, Suite 200, Lanham, Maryland 20706
www.rowman.com

86-90 Paul Street, London EC2A 4NE, United Kingdom

Copyright © 2022 by René O. Guillaume, Noelle Witherspoon Arnold, and Azadeh F. Osanloo

All rights reserved. No part of this book may be reproduced in any form or by any electronic or mechanical means, including information storage and retrieval systems, without written permission from the publisher, except by a reviewer who may quote passages in a review.

British Library Cataloguing in Publication Information Available

Library of Congress Cataloging-in-Publication Data

Names: Guillaume, René O., 1980– editor. | Arnold, Noelle Witherspoon, editor. | Osanloo, Azadeh F., editor.
Title: A companion guide to handbook of urban educational leadership : theory to practice / edited by René O. Guillaume, Noelle Witherspoon Arnold, Azadeh F. Osanloo.
Description: Lanham : Rowman & Littlefield, [2022] | Summary: "The Companion Guide activities will help illuminate salient theoretical concepts related to urban education and leadership"—Provided by publisher.
Identifiers: LCCN 2021037574 (print) | LCCN 2021037575 (ebook) | ISBN 9781475851571 (cloth) | ISBN 9781475851588 (paperback) | ISBN 9781475851595 (epub)
Subjects: LCSH: Education, Urban—United States. | Education, Urban—United States—Administration. | Educational leadership—United States.
Classification: LCC LC5131.G85 2022 (print) | LCC LC5131 (ebook) | DDC 370.9173/2—dc23
LC record available at https://lccn.loc.gov/2021037574
LC ebook record available at https://lccn.loc.gov/2021037575

Contents

PART I: LEADERS OF COLOR IN URBAN CONTEXT

1 Companion Article: Revisiting the Past to Inform the Present: Lessons from a Pre-*Brown* African American Leadership Paradigm   3
Sheryl J. Croft

2 Companion Article: Black School Leaders Matter: Applied Critical Leadership in a Large Urban District   9
Monique Sloan and Cristóbal Rodríguez

3 Companion Article: The Collective and Unique Contributions of Latina Urban School Leaders: Testimonios of Advocacy and Resistance   15
Melissa A. Martinez and Rosa L. Rivera-McCutchen

4 Companion Article: Are Charter Schools the Educational Promised Land for Black Leaders? Examining Rational Choice Theory in a Racialized Context   21
April L. Peters and Ain A. Grooms

5 Companion Article: An Ecological Model of the Urban Learner: The Geography of a Predominantly Black Institution and Multicampus Spaces   25
Ursula Thomas

PART II: HUMAN GEOGRAPHIES

6   Companion Article: "A Sanctuary while You're Here on Campus": From Safe/Brave Space to Places of Respite in Urban Educational Institutions and Classrooms   33
Douglas Allen and Shelby Chipman

7   Companion Article: Extreme Deprivation and Violence: Does Sustained Deprivation Exacerbate Homicide Rates in U.S. Cities beyond Deprivation's Direct (Linear) Effect?   39
Patricia L. McCall, Kenneth C. Land, Karen F. Parker, and Andrew C. Gray

PART III: ECOLOGICAL PERSPECTIVES

8   Companion Article: Supporting Teacher Leadership for Equity in Urban Schools   45
Joshua Childs, Judson Laughter, Bryant O. Best, and H. Richard Milner IV

9   Companion Article: Mission Ready: Globalization, Diversity, and Inclusion Viewed through the Experiences of Children of Military Service Members   49
Chadrhyn Pedraza

10 Companion Article: Harlem's Motherwork: A Valuable Resource for Urban School Leaders   53
Terri Watson

PART IV: URBAN KNOWLEDGE AND WAYS OF KNOWING

11 Companion Article: Critically Conscious Educational Leadership Development through the Use of Pláticas in an Agentic Learning Space   59
Brenda Rubio, Chris Milk-Bonilla, and Randy Clinton Bell

12 Companion Article: HQPE: Exploring the Role of Physical Education in Facing America's Educational Debt   63
Samuel R. Hodge, Martha James-Hassan, and Alexander Vigo-Valentín

13 Companion Article: Women's Perspectives on
    Deconstructing the Urban Ivory Tower for Black
    Women Faculty   71
    *Risha Berry, Tomika Ferguson, and
    Whitney Sherman Newcomb*

PART V: URBAN POLITICS AND EDUCATIONAL LEADERSHIP

14 Companion Article: Urban Education and Educational
    Leadership Graduate Preparation Programs: Preparing
    Graduate Students Coming from and Going into Urban
    Pre-K–12 Settings   81
    René O. Guillaume and Elizabeth C. Apodaca

15 Companion Article: Queering Urban Elementary
    Schools: Campus Leaders as Allies of Intersectionality   85
    Leanna Lucero and Angela V. E. Owens

16 Companion Article: Urban School Administrators'
    Incorporation of Student Voice/Culture and Community
    Involvement toward School Discipline in
    Middle Schools   91
    John A. Williams III and Chance W. Lewis

17 Companion Article: The Value of Asian American
    Pre-K–12 Urban Education Principals: A Human
    Resources Developmental Perspective on the Barriers and
    Opportunity Pathways for America's "Model Minority"   95
    Nicholas D. Hartlep

18 Companion Article: Understanding the Politics of Race,
    Equity, and Neoliberalism in Everyday Leadership   103
    *Sarah Diem, Anjalé D. Welton, Sarah W. Walters,
    and Shannon Paige Clark*

PART VI: TRANSNATIONALISM

19 Companion Article: Supporting Undocumented Students:
    Principals Taking Action   109
    Sofia Bahena, Brianda De Leon, and Mariela A. Rodríguez

20 Companion Article: Conceptualizing Equity in a
Borderland Language Ecology 113
Magdalena Pando

21 Companion Article: Projecting the Voices of the
Voiceless: Undocumented Students in a Southwest
Borderland K–12 School District 119
Roberto Lozano

22 Companion Article: "They Don't Even Know Me":
Effects of the Model Minority Myth on Asian American
Students in a Southwest Borderland High School 123
Jennifer Maya Haan

23 Companion Article: A Metaphor Analysis of Tragedy and
Trauma: Educational Leadership Responses to Addressing
Transnationalistic Terror and Racial Violence 127
*Azadeh F. Osanloo, Sarah Jane Baker, Kristine Andrea
Velásquez, Rick Marlatt, and Noelle Witherspoon Arnold*

About the Editors 133

About the Contributors 135

LEADERS OF COLOR IN URBAN CONTEXT

CHAPTER 1

Companion Article: Revisiting the Past to Inform the Present
Lessons from a Pre-*Brown* African American School Leadership Paradigm

Sheryl J. Croft

GOAL

The goals of this companion guide are multifaceted. The first goal is to provide school leaders with an activity to help their faculty examine and articulate their beliefs about educating the children with whom they work. In addition to focusing on teacher's independent beliefs, this activity affords school leaders a resource to construct a cohesive school-based educational belief system on which to construct school practices and activities. This activity also lays the groundwork on which to build school culture that is based on student needs. In other words, this companion guide offers school leaders an alternative to solely test-focused leadership and a way to engage faculty in meaningful discussion centered around their beliefs about educating children.

BACKGROUND

Brown v. Board was the landmark decision that ended segregation de jure in the South. Despite pejorative depictions of segregated schools during Jim Crow, evidence suggests that even though these schools were underresourced (Anderson, 1988; Jones, 1981; Noblit & Dempsey, 1996; Rodgers, 1975), they educated children based on a belief system consisting of aspirational and resistant beliefs. Aspirational beliefs were designed to prepare students instructionally to compete in a world that was not then open to them. Resistant beliefs prepared and fortified students to resist the negative and pejorative perceptions of society (Nelson & Guerra, 2013).

The student-centered pre-*Brown* African American School Leadership Paradigm (PAASLP), based on an aspirational and resistant belief system that successfully educated children during segregation, offers an alternative to the test-focused leadership models that now dominate educational leadership (Croft, Roberts, & Stenhouse, 2015). In contrast to contemporary, test-focused educational delivery models, the PAASLP prepared and encouraged students to achieve, aspire, and persevere despite lack of resources and in the face of prejudice and discrimination. Their belief system was the tool these leaders used to ensure equity-based leadership (Milner, 2006; Tillman, 2004; Walker, 2000; Wilson, Douglas, & Nganga, 2013). Given the recent segregation trends, this original paradigm affords school leaders an instrument to assess faculty beliefs about educating children and from which to form consensus around collective, school-wide beliefs and practices (Rothstein, 2013). Inasmuch as the PAASLP was used widely by school leaders during segregation to direct educational attainment for their students, this companion guide can be used to examine the beliefs and practices of contemporary school leaders and teachers with the goal of improving educational delivery.

THEORY TO PRACTICE

This companion guide acknowledges that principals and teachers have prior beliefs about the children they serve. These beliefs can be either positive or negative (Nelson & Guerra, 2013). Designed to provide a platform for discussion, it facilitates the articulation and examination of leaders' and teachers' beliefs. Because creating a positive school culture in which children thrive is fundamentally dependent on the beliefs of leaders and teachers, examining their beliefs is paramount. In this sense, this guide provides an opportunity to examine and discover school-wide beliefs and practices and can be a first step in establishing a student-centered school culture. As with the PAASLP, Parajes (1992) provides tenets about the nature of beliefs:

- "Knowledge and beliefs are inextricably intertwined" and can be powerful and affective (Parajes, 1992, p. 325).
- Beliefs as substructures must somehow be connected with the entire system (whether district or school) of educating children.
- Lip service to "I believe all children can learn" is not enough. School leaders must insist that their goals and practices align with beliefs that support the academic and affective growth of all children.

Using Parajes's (1992) belief tenets as theoretical underpinnings and filtered through the PASSLP, this companion guide (1) provides school leaders and teachers with a leadership alternative focused on all aspects of a student's growth and (2) supports discussions designed to assess beliefs about leadership and teaching practices and goals.

ACTIVITIES

The following activities can be conducted with whole faculties or in small groups. Roles: (1) designate a recorder who should record the group's interactions and decisions and (2) designate a reporter should call out the beliefs.

Steps in the Activity

A. Discuss belief tenets: Provide faculty tenets of beliefs, listed below.
  1. "Educational beliefs must be understood in terms of their connections not only to each other . . . but also to other, perhaps more central beliefs in the system" (Parajes, 1992, p. 325).
  2. "Beliefs are instrumental in defining tasks and selecting cognitive tools with which to interpret, plan, and make decisions regarding such tasks . . . hence, they play a critical role in defining behavior" (Parajes, 1992, p. 325).

B. Open discussion: In an "open discussion," faculty will discuss the importance of beliefs about educating children and the importance of an educational organization working from the same set of beliefs. Divergent opinions are welcome.

C. Identifying beliefs and practices about educating children (based on the two tenets listed above):
   1. Each group will construct a definition of their fundamental beliefs about educating children.
   2. Using the chart below, the faculty groups should list their beliefs about the role education should play in a student's life and how to educate all children.
      For example, "I believe that education is a great equalizer." "I believe that all children should have access to equal education."
      "I believe that schools should provide wraparound services," etc.
   3. After reaching consensus, the beliefs should be placed on one side of the chart.
   4. After listing their beliefs on one side of the chart, faculty should list their practice(s) that support their beliefs for educating children in low-income, segregated communities.
   5. Have faculty discuss whether their practices align with their beliefs. If not, suggest practices that align with beliefs.
   6. Have faculty assess whether the beliefs are positive, negative, or designed to support children.

Table 1.1. Constructing Faculty Beliefs

Beliefs about Educating Children	School Practice to Support Beliefs
I believe that all children should have access to an equitable education.	

   7. Using the Aspirational and Resistant Beliefs chart from the PAASLP in the accompanying chapter, faculty will discuss, compare, reassess, and/or revise their beliefs and practices.
   8. Each group will share and post their beliefs and practices associated with their beliefs on charts.

D. Identifying school-wide belief system
   a. Faculty as a whole will walk around the charts and place sticky notes numbered 1 to 5 with 1 representing the top priority and 5 the lowest.
   b. A designee will collect and collate the priorities.
   c. At a subsequent meeting, the collected beliefs and practices will be distributed and discussed with faculty.

REFLECTION

Using the historical and contemporary belief systems, (1) discuss the power and usefulness of this activity in identifying beliefs and practices related to educating the population of children you serve and (2) discuss the importance of identifying and institutionalizing a school belief system around educating children in general and your school's population of children specifically.

REFERENCES

Anderson, J. (1988). *The education of Blacks in the South, 1860–1935*. Chapel Hill: University of North Carolina Press.

Croft, S. J., Roberts, M. A., & Stenhouse, V. (2015). The perfect storm of education reform: High stakes testing and teacher evaluation. *Social Justice: A Journal of Crime, Conflict, and World Order, 42*(1), 70–91.

Jones, F. C. (1981). *A traditional model of educational excellence: Dunbar High School of Little Rock, Arkansas*. Washington, DC: Howard University Press.

Milner, (2006). The promise of Black teachers' success with Black students. *Educational Foundations, 20*(3–4), 89–104.

Nelson, P. L., & Guerra, S. W. (2013). Changing professional practices requires beliefs. *Phi Delta Kappan, 90*(5), 354–360.

Noblit, G. W., & Dempsey, V. O. (1996). *The social construction of virtue: The moral life of schools*. New York: New York University Press.

Parajes, F. M. (1992). Teacher's beliefs and educational research: Cleaning up a messy construct. *Review of Educational Research, 62*(3), 307–332.

Rodgers, F. A. (1975). *The African American high school and its community*. Lexington, MA: Lexington Books, D.C. Heath.

Rothstein, R. (2013). Report for public schools, segregation then, segregation since: Education and the unfinished march. *Economic Policy Institute*. https://www.epi.org/publication/unfinished-march-public-school-segregation.

Tillman, L. C. (2004). (Un)Intended consequences? The impact of *Brown v. Board of Education* decision on the employment status of Black educators. *Education and Urban Society*, *36*(3), 280–303.

Walker, V. S. (2000). Valued segregated schools for African American children in the South, 1935–1969: A review of common themes. *Review of Educational Research*, *70*(3), 253–285.

Wilson, C. M., Douglas, T. M. O., & Nganga, C. W. (2013). Starting with African American Success: A strength-based approach to transformative educational leadership. In L. C. Tillman & J. J. Scheurick (Eds.), *Handbook of research on educational leadership for equity and diversity* (pp. 111–133). New York: Routledge.

CHAPTER 2

Companion Article: Black School Leaders Matter

Applied Critical Leadership in a Large Urban District

Monique Sloan and Cristóbal Rodríguez

GOAL

The purpose of this exercise is to learn more about Black principals' usage of applied critical leadership across a large urban context. It also looks at how individuals not identifying with one or more marginalized groups can be intentional in their leadership to support the staff and students within their schools. One will examine different leadership actions and think about ways that Black principals use their lived experiences to advocate for the marginalized students within their building. This exercise will also push the thinking of the participants to engage in dialogue regarding the ways color-blindness theories, deficit perspectives, Black feminism, and transformational leadership impact majority-minority schools.

BACKGROUND

School demographics in large urban districts are rapidly changing across the United States. This change in school demographics has become a challenge to educational leaders that serve culturally and linguistically diverse students. Research suggests that principals have a deep effect on student learning and the retention of quality teachers (Khalifa, Gooden, & Davis, 2016). Research also finds that principals have the ability to influence teacher learning, shape the climate, and impact student achievement (Khalifa et al., 2016). Marginalized groups of students struggle socially and academically within a school culture that disproportionately disciplines and approaches them from a deficit-thinking perspective (Khalifa et al., 2016). School policies continue to require school leaders to address myriad problems within their schools, while the accountability measures continue to increase and school demographics continue to change. School leaders in large urban districts are faced with creating environments that are culturally responsive and that celebrate the cultural and social capital of the minority students attending their schools (Khalifa et al., 2016). School leaders must have the ability to recognize how racism and oppression are ingrained within the U.S. education system. They must possess the skills to challenge the oppression of marginalized groups within their schools while simultaneously facilitating critical conversations on race, culture, and community (Darling-Hammond, LaPointe, Meyerson, Orr, & Cohen, 2007; Khalifa, 2012; Khalifa et al., 2016).

According to the National Center for Educational Statistics (NCES) (2011), 80% of all school principals in the United States were White and non-Hispanic. Therefore, the majority of the schools located within the United States are led by individuals who may have difficulty relating to the communities they serve. While the expectations are for school leaders in urban districts to be transformational and instructional, their level of preparation continues to lack the level of preparation and rigor needed meet the current demands and expectations of being educational leaders in today's schools (Khalifa et al., 2016). Educational scholars such as Theoharis (2007) and Orr (2011) suggest that leaders must practice social justice leadership in order to advocate for marginalized groups of students in their schools. However, Darling-Hammond et al. (2007) posit that there is a lack of quality preparation programs that prepare leaders to lead in large majority-minority schools with a staff that differs in race, culture, and class. There is a growing body of literature that examines how school leaders of color positively impact the students within their organization. This small body of research tells counter-stories to the narratives about children of color and their success in the schools they attend. To that end, there is an even smaller body of research that examines how individuals utilize the positive attributes of their identity to lead in large urban districts (Santamaria, 2013). Currently, a gap in the literature exists in regard to leaders who identify with one or more marginalized groups and their impact on student success

(Murtadha & Watts, 2005; Santamaria, 2013). Significant research must be done to tell the narrative of student success in public schools.

School districts continue to grow and change demographically, while the staff in large urban districts continues to be largely White middle-class women. Students who are culturally and linguistically diverse continue to underperform compared to their Caucasian counterparts. This underperformance of students of color makes them more susceptible to early pregnancy, a great chance of dropping out of school, gang activity, and early entrance into the criminal justice system. The underperformance of students of color continues to be pervasive across the United States and must be examined in a new and critical way. This includes providing narratives that tell the stories of student success and the positive attributes leaders of color bring to their organizations that promote student success, which, currently, are barely existent.

THEORY TO PRACTICE

Compare and contrast the differences between applied critical leadership and social justice leadership. Explain why a principal may benefit from understanding and applying the strategies indicative of applied critical leadership in a large urban context.

ACTIVITIES

Given that applied critical leadership is a newer theory within the educational context, conduct research to explain why this particular theory expands one's understanding of critical race theory and transformational leadership.

1. Research at least three principal preparation programs (predominantly White institutions, historically black colleges and universities, online Universities). Analyze the program to determine the quality of the internship for administrative interns as well as the program as a whole. Pay special attention to the classes required to develop cultural competency, an equity stance, and an advocacy lens for underserved populations. Make sure to examine the

courses required for graduation versus the courses students can elect to take. Offer a critique of the program and include suggestions to help improve the quality of the program, if applicable.
2. Research one highly successful Black principal and one highly successful White male principal in large urban contexts. Compare and contrast their journey as principals. What types of things did they to do to become successful principals? Prepare a presentation chronicling their journeys. What are the commonalities? How did their journeys differ? What lessons can you learn and apply to your own journey?
3. Given the "Trump" effect, what types of difficulties might a middle-aged Caucasian male encounter entering into his first year as the principal of a large urban majority-minority school? This principal spent the majority of his career in a non-Title 1 school where 75% of the population were middle-class White families. He attended a large, diverse university where he received a full athletic scholarship for basketball. He is currently engaged to a middle-class biracial female. Prepare a first 100-day entry plan for him, using the demographics of a large urban district in your area. This plan will need to include an analysis of the school's demographic data and its academic achievement data. Be sure to include how he will engage stakeholders and build relationships within the school. Think about fiscal implications, the school culture, professional learning, and building his own capacity to ensure a successful first 100 days.

REFLECTION

Given the rapidly changing demographic across public schools in America and the changing expertise of the teaching force, how did your perspective shift and change when thinking about the struggles of a novice principal leading a large urban school?

Historically, Black principals have played an integral role in mentoring and supporting the upcoming teaching force. They served as mentors and supports to the teachers as well as to the students in their care. Currently, there is a shortage of teachers, especially Black males and Latinx teachers. With that being said, after *Brown v. Board of Educa-*

tion, there was a mass exodus of Black principals due to demotions and firings. How might districts leverage their recruitment and staffing efforts to recruit minority principals and educators? How can minority principals benefit the communities and students they serve?

REFERENCES

Darling-Hammond, L., LaPointe, M., Meyerson, D., Orr, M. T., & Cohen, C. (2007). *Preparing school leaders for a changing world: Lessons from exemplary leadership development programs*. Stanford, CA: Stanford University, Stanford Educational Leadership Institute.

Khalifa, M. (2012). A re-new-ed paradigm in successful urban school leadership: Principal as community leader. *Educational Administration Quarterly, 48*(3), 424–467.

Khalifa, M. A., Gooden, M. A., & Davis, J. E. (2016). Culturally responsive school leadership: A synthesis of the literature. *Review of Educational Research, 86*(4), 1272–1311.

Murtadha, K., & Watts, D. M. (2005). Linking the struggle for education and social justice: Historical perspectives of African American leadership in schools. *Educational Administration Quarterly, 42*(4), 591–608.

Orr, M. T. (2011). Pipeline to preparation to advancement: Graduates' experiences in, through, and beyond leadership preparation. *Educational Administration Quarterly, 74*(1), 114–172.

Santamaria, L. (2013). Critical change for the greater good: Multicultural perceptions in educational leadership toward social justice and equity. *Educational Administration Quarterly, 50*(3), 347–391.

Theoharis, G. (2007). Social justice educational leaders and resistance: Toward a theory of social justice leadership. *Educational Administration Quarterly, 43*(2), 221–258.

ADDITIONAL RESOURCES

- National Center for Educational Statistics
    https://nces.ed.gov
- Baltimore City Public Schools
    https://www.baltimorecityschools.org
- Houston Identified School District
    https://www.houstonisd.org

CHAPTER 3

Companion Article: The Collective and Unique Contributions of Latina Urban School Leaders

Testimonios of Advocacy and Resistance

Melissa A. Martinez and Rosa L. Rivera-McCutchen

GOAL

The intent of this guide is to help readers extend and apply concepts and findings presented in the accompanying chapter to gain a deeper understanding of the assets of and challenges faced by Latina urban school leaders. The tasks promote greater self-awareness and provide practice for considering ways to strengthen opportunities to increase and sustain the representation of Latinas in critical school and district leadership roles.

BACKGROUND

Most Latina school principals are leading in urban contexts, yet their contributions to urban school communities across the country are minimally documented and often on the periphery of mainstream urban educational leadership literature (Gonzales, Ulloa, & Muñoz, 2016; Hernandez & Murakami, 2016a; Méndez-Morse, Murakami, Byrne-Jiménez, & Hernandez, 2015). Latina school leaders can be considered key assets because of their cultural, linguistic, and gendered identities, which contribute to their ability to build strong ties with families and communities and relate authentically to students of color (Loebe, 2004; Martinez, Rivera, & Marquez, 2019; Palacio, 2013). Yet these same characteristics that can afford them opportunities for advancement can often become a double-edged sword that can lead to them being underestimated, stereotyped, and/or pigeonholed (Hernandez & Murakami, 2016b).

The testimonios of the Latina urban leaders in the chapter reiterate and extend some of these previous findings. The Latina leaders contributed to their communities by advocating for others given their own inequitable experiences. They built capacity and community, although this was often in isolation. They also developed political acumen in an effort to avoid or respond to hostility they encountered in their roles. The strengths of the participants as well as tensions they experienced were distinctly shaped by their individual intersectional identities and experiences and the contexts in which they worked. This underscores the need for a deeper understanding of the experiences of Latina leaders in order to strengthen future recruitment and retention efforts.

THEORY TO PRACTICE

Intersectionality was the lens used to analyze the testimonios of Elida, Cindy, and Nora to uncover how their experiences were shaped by their multiple social identities and how various systems of power functioned to oppress them. Thus, an intersectional lens is useful to examine the complexity of our own positionalities and social identities as well as those of whom we work with and serve, especially our students (Carey, Yee, & DeMatthews, 2018). Identify your own multiple and intersecting identities and consider how you can utilize an intersectionality lens to better understand and serve the students and families in your school community.

ACTIVITIES

1. Treating each Latina leader's story in this chapter as a case study, apply relevant educational leadership theories and frameworks to identify practical solutions to the challenges the women faced in their urban settings. Some relevant frameworks include social justice leadership (Rivera-McCutchen, 2014; Ryan, 2010; Theoharis, 2010), culturally relevant leadership (Horsford, Grosland, & Gunn, 2011; Khalifa, 2018), and applied critical leadership (Santamaria & Santamaria, 2012).

2. Draw on data from local urban school districts or data from one urban school district within your state/region to develop a district plan for strengthening the Latina leadership pipeline or building a more racially/ethnically diverse leadership pipeline.

REFLECTION

Considered methodological, pedagogical, and political tools, testimonios center the voices and experiences of oppressed individuals and communities (Blackmer Reyes & Curry Rodríguez, 2012; Delgado Bernal, Burciaga, & Carmona, 2012). Testimonios can therefore be useful to document one's own experiences or those of others, serving as sources of knowledge and reflection. To delve into this methodological tool for further reflection, write a two- to three-page testimonio documenting your educational and career trajectory, highlighting critical incidents in which you personally felt marginalized or witnessed students, parents, or educators being marginalized or treated inequitably. Document how you reacted in such instances and if and how you addressed the injustices.

REFERENCES

Blackmer Reyes, K., & Curry Rodríguez, J. E. (2012). Testimonio: Origins, terms, and Resources. *Equity and Excellence in Education, 45*(3), 525–538.

Carey, R. L., Yee, L. S., & DeMatthews, D. (2018). Power, penalty, and critical praxis: Employing intersectionality in educator practices to achieve school equity. *The Educational Forum, 82*(1), 111–130.

Delgado Bernal, D., Burciaga, R., & Carmona, J. F. (2012). Chicana/Latina testimonios: Mapping the methodological, pedagogical, and political. *Equity & Excellence in Education, 45*(3), 363–372.

Gonzales, S. M., Ulloa, A. M., & Muñoz, C. (2016). "CEO's don't cry." "But, this one does": Gender identity, language and culture at the periphery of school leadership in Latina/o Detroit. *National Forum of Educational Administration and Supervision Journal, 33*(2–3), 29–41.

Hernandez, F., & Murakami, E. T. (2016a). *Brown-eyed leaders of the sun: A portrait of Latina/o educational leaders.* Charlotte, NC: Information Age Publishing.

Hernandez, F., & Murakami, E. T. (2016b). Counterstories about leadership: A Latina school principal's experience from a less documented view in an urban school context. *Educational Sciences, 6*(6), 1–16.

Horsford, S. D., Grosland, T., & Gunn, K. M. (2011). Pedagogy of the personal and professional: Toward a framework for culturally relevant leadership. *Journal of School Leadership, 21*, 582–606.

Khalifa, M. (2018). *Culturally responsive school leadership.* Cambridge, MA: Harvard Education Press.

Loebe, A. Y. (2004). *Educational leadership for school change: Stories by six Latina elementary school principals.* Unpublished doctoral dissertation, University of Arizona, Tucson.

Martinez, M. A., Rivera, M., & Marquez, J. (2019). Learning from the experiences and development of Latina school leaders. *Educational Administration Quarterly*, 1–27. doi:10.1177/0013161X19866491

Méndez-Morse, S., Murakami, E. T., Byrne-Jiménez, M., & Hernandez, F. (2015). Mujeres in the principal's office: Latina school leaders. *Journal of Latinos and Education, 14*(3), 171–187.

Palacio, C. A. (2013). *The career development of Latina women achieving the position of public high school principal.* Unpublished doctoral dissertation, University of Wisconsin, Milwaukee.

Rivera-McCutchen, R. L. (2014). The moral imperative of social justice leadership: A critical component of effective practice. *The Urban Review, 46*(40), 747–763. https://doi.org/10.1007/s11256-014-0297-2

Ryan, J. (2010). Promoting social justice in schools: Principals' political strategies. *International Journal of Leadership in Education: Theory and Practice, 13*(4), 357–376.

Santamaria, L. J., & Santamaria, A. P. (2012). *Applied critical leadership in education: Choosing change.* New York: Routledge.

Theoharis, G. (2010). Disrupting injustice: Principals narrate the strategies they use to improve their schools and advance social justice. *Teachers College Record, 112*(1), 331–373.

ADDITIONAL RESOURCES

- Strengthening the Principal Pipeline: Innovate Ideas from State Equity Plans
    https://gtlcenter.org/blog/strengthening-principal-pipeline-innovative-ideas-state-equity-plans

- Teaching at the Intersections: Honor and Teach about Your Students' Multiple Identities
  https://www.tolerance.org/magazine/summer-2016/teaching-at-the-intersections
- University of Michigan—Inclusive Teaching: Social Identity Wheel
  https://sites.lsa.umich.edu/inclusive-teaching/2017/08/16/social-identity-wheel

CHAPTER 4

Companion Article: Are Charter Schools the Educational Promised Land for Black Leaders?

Examining Rational Choice Theory in a Racialized Context

April L. Peters and Ain A. Grooms

GOAL

The purpose of this companion guide is to provide aspiring leaders opportunities for reflection and planning particularly with respect to choice and reform. Charters are a reform that are prevalent in urban settings. Leaders need to understand the research, policies, and practices that underpin the experiences of parents and their children within the charter school context.

BACKGROUND

Charter schools are typically located in urban contexts and enroll students of color, particularly African American and Latinx. Charters offer parents and students choice, although the research on charter student performance indicates that there is no significant difference between charter and traditional school student outcomes. For Black students and leaders, though, the appeal of charters may be different than that of their White counterparts.

Black educators—teachers and leaders—have a positive and significant impact on the academic success of Black children. Critical race theory reminds us that without an emphasis on race, the educational needs of students of color are not likely served by their schools (Ladson-Billings & Tate, 1995). This is especially important because school choice studies are generally color blind (Cooper, 2005). Further, rational choice theory suggests that individuals act in their own best interests (Heath, 1976; McClendon, 1985), but critics contend that people do not act rationally but instead are driven by emotion, habit, or impulse (Hechter & Kanazawa, 1997). School choice research suggests that parents wield their political, economic, social, and cultural capital (Bosetti, 2004) to ensure that their children obtain the best educational opportunities and outcomes (Boone & Van Houtte, 2013; Lyken-Segosebe & Hinz, 2015).

THEORY TO PRACTICE

In this guide, readers will consider critical race theory and rational choice theory, as well as the intersection of both, in leading Black students and working with their parents on the following activities. Your responses should be grounded in your knowledge and understanding of the related research and your practical experiences.

ACTIVITIES

1. Identify the differences between schooling experiences in traditional schools and charters for marginalized groups. What can each context learn from the other? Develop a parent guidebook that reflects this learning and communicates it effectively to parent stakeholders.
2. Research other marginalized groups (race, ability, gender, sexuality, language, and so on) and examine parents' rationale in selecting traditional school or school choice options.
3. Develop a plan to identify and understand the schooling needs and desires of marginalized groups (which are often decidedly different from their White middle-class counterparts) in urban settings:
    a. How will you collect "data"?
    b. What will implementation look like (i.e., professional learning, parent informational nights, community meetings, and so on)? Be specific.
    c. Develop a plan to assess/evaluate and revise.

REFLECTION

Apply a critical lens to rational choice theory (as articulated in this chapter) as you deliberate on your responses to the following questions that focus on race, choice, and education:

1. Why do Black parents make particular educational choices for their children? What is happening in charters that meets Black parents' vision of education for their children? What is happening in traditional schools?
2. How should urban school leaders integrate their professional responsibilities (policy, achievement, and funding) with the needs/interests of their constituents (Black parents/families)?
3. What should an urban school leader do to ensure that parents remain in his or her school (traditional or choice) as opposed to opting out in favor of a more "appropriate" option?
4. Given the notion that public education is "for all," how do choice options provide competing visions of the purpose of schooling for different groups in urban settings? How could/should traditional schooling contexts be transmogrified in order to meet the needs of diverse student groups?

REFERENCES

Boone, S., & Van Houtte, M. (2013). In search of the mechanisms conducive to class differentials in educational choice: A mixed method research. *Sociological Review, 61*(3), 549–572.

Bossetti, L. (2004). Determinants of school choice: Understanding how parents choose elementary schools in Alberta. *Journal of Education Policy, 19*(4), 387–405.

Cooper, C. W. (2005). School choice and the standpoint of African American mothers: Considering the power of positionality. *Journal of Negro Education, 74*(2), 174–189.

Heath, A. (1976). *Rational choice and social exchange: A critique of exchange theory.* Oxford, UK: Oxford University Press.

Hechter, M., & Kanazawa, S. (1997). Sociological rational choice theory. *American Sociological Review, 23*, 191–214.

Ladson-Billings, G., & Tate, W. F. (1995). Toward a critical race theory of education. *Teachers College Record*, *97*(1), 47–68.

Lyken-Segosebe, D., & Hinz, S. E. (2015). The politics of parental involvement: How opportunity hoarding and prying shape educational opportunity. *Peabody Journal of Education*, *90*(1), 93–112.

McClendon, M. J. (1985). Racism, rational choice, and white opposition to racial change: A case study of busing. *Public Opinion Quarterly*, *49*(2), 214–233.

ADDITIONAL RESOURCES

- Brookings Brown Center Chalkboard
  https://www.brookings.edu/blog/brown-center-chalkboard/2019/05/21/democrats-views-on-charters-diverge-by-race-as-2020-elections-loom
- Hechinger Report
  https://hechingerreport.org/opinion-charter-school-parent-on-democratic-candidates-for-president/
- Fresno State Digital Repository
  http://repository.library.fresnostate.edu/bitstream/handle/10211.3/193746/Morris_csu_6050D_10431.pdf
- Public Charter Schools
  https://www.publiccharters.org/taxonomy/term/153

CHAPTER 5

Companion Article:
An Ecological Model of the Urban Learner

The Geography of a Predominantly Black Institution and Multicampus Spaces

Ursula Thomas

GOAL

The purpose of this activity is to engage the reader about additional factors that influence or impact the journey of the African American male as teacher. This activity will engage the reader in examining multiple factors that influence the teacher pipeline for African American males and provide illumination to practices that bolster the presence of the African American male in educator preparation program as well as overall general college success. This activity will engage the reader in identifying proper support as well as recruitment and retention practices for African American males in the teacher pipeline.

BACKGROUND

Education is a gauge of any community's advancement and improvement, but it has particular consequences in African American populations. It determines economic advancement and access to other opportunities, such as food security, financial security, and career mobility. As education is vital and everyone recognizes its worth, it still continues to have a destructive influence on African Americans for many reasons. There are two issues that secede all others: the educational system and safety (Gunn & Morris, 2013; Irvin, Byun, Meece, Reed, & Farmer, 2016).

During the past 20 years, African American students nationally have made tangible advances in academic achievement. Nevertheless, too many African American students still are not getting the excellent education they require and warrant, and the performance of African American learners trail behind that of White learners. These differences in achievement are propelled by disparities in opportunity—African American students have less of the school resources and understandings that are known to provide academic proficiency (Madyun, 2011).

Based on the research of African American male students, obstacles and achievement gaps in higher education are owed to a multifaceted group of dynamics ranging from societal discriminatory systems to local economic cuts in programs associated with being a member of this specific social group (Fullard, 2020). Disparities in race and class, shortage of role models and advocates, communities with continuing unemployment, and high levels of segregation all play a part (Gavins, 2009).

The issue of student success and the African American male as part of the journey through the teacher pipeline has gained traction over the past 20 years but is still relatively young in the world of curriculum and instruction research (Byrd et al., 2011; Goings & Bianco, 2016; U.S. Department of Education, 2016). According to data from Tolliver and Miller (2018), continued shortages of college completion by African American males as well as the remarkably low numbers of African American males in teacher education programs remain as exacerbated problems and issues (Albert Shanker Institute, 2015; Simmons, 2010). Currently, the percentage of Black male teachers in the United States is 2 percent of the total teacher population in the United States (Riser-Kositsky, 2019).

THEORY TO PRACTICE

Identify sociocultural frameworks that could undergird the college completion rates of African American males and specifically African American males who are in educator preparation programs. Some of these frameworks are critical race theory, masculinity theory, cultural theory, and social identity theory (Brown, 2009, 2011).

ACTIVITIES

1. Conduct an interview with a retired African American male educator and sociocultural historian with a background in the Black experience in the twentieth century to learn more about the sociocultural influences on Black teacher identity and its importance in a public school setting.
2. Conduct interviews with a small group of African American male teachers who have been teaching five years or less and are identified in the novice teacher category. Ask them to identify their greatest challenges and their greatest accomplishments in their careers thus far. It would be important to note which factors influence their retention in the field.
3. Identify five organizations that support the African American male teacher pipeline and retention efforts. Be sure to find out more about their mission, goals, objectives, and corporate and nonprofit partnerships along with university partnerships to increase their presence and their service areas.
4. Identify a mental health professional who specifically works with African American males. Investigate the environmental stressors that weigh heavily on the definition of success as an African American male in developing his identity and resilience factor.

REFLECTION

In many settings, African American males are viewed from a deficit perspective, and because of that, they are often not provided the developmentally and culturally appropriate support mechanisms to assist in their success. Think about your own view of appropriate supports to aid in the academic success of African American males in the education pipeline. What did you learn through the exercises about the appropriateness for the very specific needs in support of African American males in their educational experience?

African American males and their educational journey need very specific support at developmental milestones in their academic journey. Tailoring support is essential in meeting their needs. This includes ongoing mentoring as well as sociopsychological support in developing their identity as well as their resilience. This means tailoring mentoring programs and tutoring programs as well as the academic advising that they receive through high school counselors as well as through academic advisers in their collegiate pursuits. How can we as an educational community provide opportunities tailored specifically to African American males in an intentional way?

The need for additional support for African American males and subsequently the pipeline of African American male teachers requires a very specific and nuanced approach. Contrary to popular belief, members within the African American community have long identified this need. In a grassroots effort, they have responded to the needs of this particular population, but it is not enough. It must be a national effort. Based on the current programs and resources that are provided, how can we multiply and increase the support of his population with the programs that have been modeled? How can we make these programs more of the "norm" and make them mainstreamed and revered as best practices?

REFERENCES

Albert Shanker Institute. (2015). *The state of teacher diversity in American education*. Washington, DC: Albert Shanker Institute.

Brown, A. L. (2009). "O brotha where art thou?" Examining the ideological discourses of African American male teachers working with African American male students. *Race Ethnicity and Education, 12*(4), 473–493.

Brown, A. L. (2011). Pedagogies of experience: A case of the African American male teacher. *Teaching Education, 22*(4), 363–376.

Byrd, D. A., Butler, B. R., Lewis, C. W., Bonner, F. A., Rutledge, M., & Watson, J. J. (2011). Identifying new sources of African American male preservice teachers: Creating a path from student-athlete to student-teacher. *Journal of Negro Education, 80*(3), 384–397.

Fullard, D. A. (2020). Educational social justice in action through the Black Male Initiative (BMI) program. *New Directions for Adult and Continuing Education, 164*, 121–133.

Gavins, R. (2009). A historical view of the barriers faced by Black American males in pursuit of higher education. *Diversity in Higher Education, 6*, 13–29.

Goings, R. B., & Bianco, M. (2016). It's hard to be who you don't see: An exploration of Black male high school students' perspectives on becoming teachers. *Urban Review, 48*(4), 628–646.

Gunn, M. V., & Morris, C. L. (2013). A call for African American male teachers: The supermen expected to solve the problems of low-performing schools. In Lewis, C. W., & Toldson, I. A. (Eds.), *Black male teachers: Advances in Race and Ethnicity in Education* (Vol. 1, pp. 151–165). Bingley, UK: Emerald Publishing.

Irvin, M. J., Byun, S., Meece, J. L., Reed, K. S., & Farmer, T. W. (2016). School characteristics and experiences of African American, Hispanic/Latino, and Native American youth in rural communities: Relation to educational aspirations. *Peabody Journal of Education, 91*(2), 176–202.

Madyun, N. H. (2011). Connecting social disorganization theory to African-American outcomes to explain the achievement gap. *Educational Foundations, 25,* 21–35.

Riser-Kositsky, M. (2019, January 3). *Education statistics: Facts about American schools.* https://www.edweek.org/ew/issues/education-statistics/index.html.

Simmons, R. W., III. (2010). Pursuing racial equity in our schools: Lessons Learned from African American male teachers in a suburban school district. *Ailacte Journal, 7,* 33–47.

Tolliver, D. V., III, & Miller, M. T. (2018). Graduation 101: Critical strategies for African American men college completion. *Education, 138*(4), 301–308.

U.S. Department of Education. (2016). *The state of racial diversity in the educator workforce.* Washington, DC: U.S. Department of Education.

ADDITIONAL RESOURCES

- Welcome to Call Me MISTER®
    https://www.clemson.edu/education/research/programs/call memister
- My Brother's Keeper
    https://obamawhitehouse.archives.gov/my-brothers-keeper
- The Campaign for Black Male Achievement (CBMA)
    https://www.Blackmaleachievement.org
- The State of Racial Diversity in the Educator Workforce
    https://www.ed.gov/news/press-releases/report-state-racial-diversity-educator-workforce

- Profound Gentlemen
  https://www.profoundgentlemen.org
- Keeping Black Men in Front of the Class
  https://www.npr.org/sections/ed/2015/10/20/446858885/keeping-Black-men-in-front-of-the-class
- Black and Hispanic/Latino Male Teachers Initiative Networked Improvement Community
  https://aacte.org/programs-and-services/nic
- Brothers Empowered to Teach Initiative
  https://wkkf.org/grants/grant/2018/11/building-a-pipeline-of-Black-male-educators-and-expanding-quality-alternative-certification-provider
- Project Pipeline Repair: Restoring Minority Male Participation and Persistence in Educator Preparation Program
  https://sheeo.org/project/project-pipeline-repair-restoring-minority-male-participation-and-persistence-in-educator-preparation-programs

Part II

HUMAN GEOGRAPHIES

CHAPTER 5

Companion Article: "A Sanctuary while You're Here on Campus"

From Safe/Brave Space to Places of Respite in Urban Educational Institutions and Classrooms

Douglas Allen and Shelby Chipman

GOAL

Through this section, we hope to connect the conceptual analytic of *places of respite* to the practice of producing places of respite in your own schools. We will provide a few general suggestions to get started in (re)producing our schools and classrooms as places of respite; ask a set of questions meant to guide educational leaders to evaluate the practices and culture being produced in their schools and to encourage implementation of inclusive, justice-oriented practices; and offer a few recommended readings to continue engaging with social justice education. We encourage leaders to embrace the spirit of the *places of respite* concept and make this a collaborative activity and to share both your successes and areas of growth with colleagues, faculty, staff, parents, and students.

BACKGROUND

Places of respite are produced within particular contexts and, thus, will differ from school to school and even from classroom to classroom. Because they are produced by the students, faculty, and staff in these places, a variety of specialized strategies will be required to address the desires and concerns of those using these places. Indeed, this diversity of concerns will be true within our schools as well. As a result, one of the first things we can do to produce affirmative places of respite is to produce smaller-scale places of respite for subgroups of students.

These places are simultaneously separate places of respite and part of the production of the school as a place of respite. These places, such as a room before or after school for LGBTQ students to organize and affirm each other, help produce the school as a place of respite. We must be vigilant, however, that these smaller-scale places of respite do not become the only place these students are affirmed. If that occurs, then the school ceases to be a place of respite and instead becomes a place one needs respite from.

THEORY TO PRACTICE

- *Establish trust.* We need to return radical honesty to our schools. We must be more transparent with students, faculty, and the community. Make informing and receiving comments and concerns from the students and faculty a practice. Begin a practice of "questions, comments, concerns" to allow students and faculty to clarify, provide feedback, and question decisions.
- *Evaluate your school's culture.* Have a meeting with students, staff, and faculty in small groups to discuss the school and classroom cultures and what burdens and anxieties you can work to relieve. You might also expand this evaluation to include how your school and school population culture includes or impacts the broader community.
- *Evaluate your curriculum.* To create an affirmative curriculum, we must ensure that our instruction resonates with students' lived experience and is social justice oriented. Demand that resonant instruction be part of each educator's lesson plans and make sure that your curriculum includes engagement with the community and community needs.
- *Create a culture of stewardship.* Have students participate in the design, implementation, and maintenance of your school's classrooms, halls, and external landscapes. If possible, have students decorate and maintain the parts of the school near the site of their social group's space (e.g., the band room for band students).
- *Create places for (self-)care and healing.* Make space and time for healing in your school through various courses, sites, and

designated times for your students to discuss issues and concerns important to them. Encourage students to share their stories in these places and encourage a supportive culture within the school, having faculty lead by example.
- *Reconceptualize discipline as justice.* Eliminate disciplinary referrals and disciplinary officers and adopt a system of sending students to counselors who have been trained in restorative justice or conflict mediation. This is a first step; eventually, the goal is to have training in restorative justice for all students and faculty and to implement a full restorative justice approach.
- *Forge relationships with community partners.* These should not be the corporate, school-to-capitalism relationships but rather service relationships within the community to connect our instruction with engagement in the real world. Make these true partnerships where students engage in service within the community and where community members are brought into the classroom or school as experts.

ACTIVITIES

This activity section asks you to engage in an organizational type of "think-pair-share" exercise: *think* about the questions/provocations below; *pair* with colleagues, faculty, staff, parents, and students to get their perspective and to swap ideas; and *share* your ideas and goals gathered and developed through this exercise with your school and begin to shape your school as a place that shares the responsibility of creating an inclusive, justice-oriented environment and society.

Guiding Questions

1. Whose school and/or classroom *is* it?
    a. Whose vision and experiences are legible in your school, and whose are invisibilized?
    b. How are you making sure that students are stewards of your school and feel a sense responsibility for it as their place?

2. What relations of relief do your students, faculty, and/or staff desire or require?
   a. What are you doing in your school and classrooms to relieve the anxiety and burdens your students, faculty, and staff experience within society?
   b. How is your disciplinary structure contributing to or dismantling cultures of punishment and fear?
3. What is your school doing to encourage and facilitate self-care and healing (beyond school counselors)?
   a. How are you encouraging a culture of responsibility that creates a supportive atmosphere?
   b. Do you provide opportunities for students to express their emotions within a supportive group?
4. How are you producing your school to visually, audibly, and emotionally affirm your students' identities and experiences?
   a. How much of your educational curriculum resonates with the lived experiences of your students?
   b. Which students in your school are least affirmed? Why and how can you (re)make this place to affirm those students?
5. What is the point of your discipline structure?
   a. Is it a punishment and deterrence strategy, or is it meant to restore harmonious, collaborative community relations?
   b. Does your discipline structure (intentionally or unintentionally) separate and ostracize offenders from the community, or are offenders encouraged to ask forgiveness and make amends through acts while part of the community?

REFLECTION

It is incumbent on all of us (students, staff, faculty, and educational/community leaders) to create spaces that affirm each of our lives and perspectives and that facilitate an inclusive, justice-oriented society. This begins with those who have the capacity to make meaningful changes in our (educational) institutions, such as educational leaders, but must include all stakeholders in our institutions (students, staff, faculty, educational leaders, parents, and community members). It can be productive to establish student and staff councils in addition to the faculty council you may already have and to establish a way to gather, evaluate, and act on the information, concerns, and needs expressed from these councils. It is important that these councils are taken seriously by participants, educators, and educational leaders. These are not perfunctory or frivolous bureaucracies. They should be core to the way we evaluate and change our institutions. We must be self-critical and see change not as an indictment of ourselves or our prior modus operandi. Instead, opportunities for change must be seen as learning moments, as teachable moments, and as part of a larger project of an ongoing pursuit of justice. Just as our pursuit of justice is never finished, our educational institutions and their constituent spaces must also always be (re)evaluated and changed to become a little more inclusive, a little more justice oriented, and a little more affirmative.

ADDITIONAL RESOURCES

- Allen, D. L. (2020). Black geographies of respite: Relief, recuperation, and resonance at Florida A&M University. *Antipode*. https://doi.org/10.1111/anti.12658
- Freire, P. (1970). *Pedagogy of the oppressed*. New York: Continuum.
- Gay, G. (2000). *Culturally responsive teaching: Theory, research, and practice*. New York: Teachers College Press.
- Gannon, K. M. (2020). *Radical hope: A teaching manifesto*. Morgantown: West Virginia University Press.
- hooks, bell. (1994). *Teaching to transgress: Education as the practice of freedom*. New York: Routledge.
- Love, B. (2019). *We want to do more than survive: Abolitionist teaching and the pursuit of educational freedom*. Boston: Beacon Press.
- Schmidt, L. (2009). "Stirring up justice." *Educational Leadership*, 66(8), 32–37.
- Wadhwa, A. (2015). *Restorative justice in urban schools: Disrupting the school-to-prison pipeline*. New York: Routledge.

- Warren, C. A., & Coles, J. (2020). Trading spaces: Antiblackness and reflections on Black education futures. *Equity and Excellence in Education.* https://doi.org/10.1080/10665684.2020.1764882.

CHAPTER 7

Companion Article: Extreme Deprivation and Violence

Does Sustained Deprivation Exacerbate Homicide Rates in U.S. Cities beyond Deprivation's Direct (Linear) Effect?

Patricia L. McCall, Kenneth C. Land, Karen F. Parker, and Andrew C. Gray

GOAL

In these exercises, the goal is to consider the real-world implication of structural forces, especially those related to the economy, that have shaped cities and levels of violent crime within them. It encourages us to examine how decisions made in economic and political realms can have major and lasting impacts on people living within American cities, such as the barriers that many confront in accessing employment opportunities and a quality education.

BACKGROUND

Our chapter in this book is the result of a long history of criminological research that has been concerned with how the social environment influences crime rates. Eventually, criminology began to focus more on individual-level theorizing and research, but macro-level theories of crime have experienced a resurgence with the advancements of several lines of inquiry, such as the focus on economic inequality/resource deprivation (Blau & Blau, 1982; Williams & Flewelling, 1988) and concentrated disadvantage (Wilson, 1987). Resource deprivation has proven to be one of the strongest and most consistent macro-level predictors of crime (Pratt & Cullen, 2005), and we built on previous works by considering extreme and sustained levels of resource deprivation across U.S. cities. Not only is resource deprivation an important predictor of homicides, but high levels of homicide are associated with extreme levels of resource deprivation across a sample of cities. While not directly examined, these extreme levels of deprivation can also impact the education system within cities (Wilson, 1996).

THEORY TO PRACTICE

In our chapter, we discuss the distribution of resource deprivation and homicides across large U.S. cities, including a sample of cities classified as having high homicide rates. This allows for anyone interested in this topic to identify one (or more) of the cities from our analysis to be examined in more depth in light of our findings. Thus, these cities can be used as real-world examples and can be examined as case studies for understanding high levels of homicide and sustained resource deprivation. We offer two exercises that illustrate the relationship between theory and practice.

ACTIVITIES

1. *City case studies.* Pick two cities—one from our sample of high-homicide cities and one outside that sample—to compare. For example, you could compare Philadelphia, Pennsylvania (one of the 66 high-homicide cities), to Columbus, Ohio. Once you have the cities selected, find information about them from the U.S. Census or visit the World Population Review website (http://worldpopulationreview.com) to make comparisons about their demographic makeup, socioeconomic characteristics, and so on. You can also track changes within these cities over time. How has the population changed? Have economic characteristics of the cities improved or worsened? Additionally, you can use data from the FBI to examine trends in crime within the cities you select. What are their differences in crime? Have homicide levels increased, decreased, or been stable in these cities? What type of policies could help address deprivation and crime?
2. *Mapping and/or visiting cities.* Select a city from our study and locate it in Google Maps. Pick a starting point and enter street view, which allows you to travel through the streets. Explore the city and look for characteristics that may represent signs of eco-

nomic deprivation. For example, you may see closed factories, vacant apartments and homes, boarded-up businesses/storefronts, and/or school buildings that appear to be lacking funding. Do some areas of the city appear to be more economically advantaged than others? What characteristics represent economic deprivation? In a YouTube video (https://www.youtube.com/watch?v=G-w6vi4Q0oM), Robert J. Sampson discussed data collection efforts that relied on "systematic social observation" where individuals examined videos taken along city streets and noted signs of "disorder" that are symptoms of larger social problems (i.e., economic inequality and segregation). This exercise represents an approximation of how this type of data collection is accomplished.

REFLECTION

While much of criminology has turned its focus on individuals and their behavior, structural forces that may be influencing the trajectories of their lives must also be considered. What our chapter has shown is that violent crime is associated with extreme and sustained levels of economic deprivation, and the exercises above were designed to help put these structural forces that have a real, detrimental impact on people residing in U.S. cities with high levels of disadvantage into a more tangible, real-world context.

REFERENCES

Blau, J., & Blau, P. (1982). Metropolitan structure and violent crime. *American Sociological Review, 47*(1), 114–128.

Pratt, T. C., & Cullen, F. T. (2005). Assessing macro-level predictors and theories of crime: A meta-analysis. *Crime and Justice, 32*, 373–450.

Williams, K. R., & Flewelling, R.L. (1988). The social production of criminal homicide: A comparative study of disaggregated rates in U.S. cities. *American Sociological Review, 53*(3), 421–431.

Wilson, W. J. (1987). *The truly disadvantaged: The inner city, the underclass and public policy*. Chicago: University of Chicago Press.

Wilson, W. J. (1996). *When work disappears: The world of the new urban poor*. New York: Vintage Books.

Part III

ECOLOGICAL PERSPECTIVES

CHAPTER 8

Companion Article: Supporting Teacher Leadership for Equity in Urban Schools

Joshua Childs, Judson Laughter, Bryant O. Best, and H. Richard Milner IV

GOAL

The goal of this companion guide is to provide insight for thinking through the type of work that is necessary for teacher leaders to engage in holistic and context-specific educational equity practices. In this companion guide, we provide information on the importance of equity-centered professional development and pedagogy.

BACKGROUND

In recent years, school districts have responded to demographic shifts affecting educational opportunity for students of color, English language learners, low-income students, and students living in poverty. Deficit thinking has persisted within educational contexts for many years and contributes to disparities in teaching and learning, academic achievement, and postsecondary readiness and success. Equitable educational opportunities should be provided for all students, no matter the school or community context, and this starts with supporting the building of dispositions, knowledge, and skills of the teachers who interact daily with students.

Urban schools serve as important hubs of knowledge and educational resources that can provide pathways for students who are often left behind or overlooked. Urban schools should be hiring faculty and implementing practices that work toward greater equity and support a commitment to social justice teaching and leadership practices.

Teacher leaders, who often serve in roles that occupy mentoring and supporting fellow teachers, can be a great conduit for educational equity in urban school settings.

THEORY TO PRACTICE

Teacher leaders need a thorough set of dispositions, knowledge, and skills to address issues of diversity and equity in urban school environments. Preservice programs and professional development services are limited in offering teacher leaders adequate resources and training that can help in addressing issues of diversity and equity (Cochran-Smith, Davis, & Fries, 2004). The limited availability of these offerings to prepare teachers to lead and teach for equity make it important to look at multiple pathways for teacher learning and growth.

Equity work can be stressful, especially for teacher leaders who are playing dual roles within their school (Lac & Diamond, 2019). Traditional notions of leadership in schools has focused more on school management and less on the inequitable practices and policies that exist in schools. Sometimes, teacher leaders exacerbate policies and activities that further marginalize students and their families, especially in urban schooling contexts. Teacher leaders should be helping to manifest an environment of equitable practices and should possess the training and skills to bring realization to this type of work. Teacher leaders should be critically questioning the inequities within their schools and working to dismantle them. Furthermore, teacher leaders should be self-reflective of their own practices and biases that help to create inequitable learning and social environments for their students.

ACTIVITIES

Self-Reflection

At the beginning of each academic term (e.g., semester, quarter, and so forth), teacher leaders should reflect on and answer these questions:

1. Who is determining what is equitable when it comes to instruction? Leadership? Professional development?

2. How am I contributing to equitable or inequitable teaching and learning opportunities for students in my school? How am I contributing to equitable or inequitable leadership policies and practices in my school?
3. What can I do, starting today, to dismantle one inequitable practice? How can I get allies on this endeavor?
4. At the end of the term, I will see equity manifesting in the following ways.
5. By the end of this academic term, students and families will be able to see equity practiced daily at this school in the following ways.

REFLECTION

Schools are complex organizations with distinct practices and policies that may impede the growth of equitable opportunities and advancement. Cultural and structural challenges, beyond teacher leaders' control, can help create a lack of formal opportunities to dismantle inequities. However, opportunities exist for teacher leaders to interrogate their own practices and beliefs as related to equity and how they are helping to shape and inform their working environment and student opportunities. Attention to the root cause of educational inequity and intentional reflection on how to dismantle these inequities are important in order to move to solutions that can provide better teaching and learning environments for students.

REFERENCES

Cochran-Smith, M., Davis, D., & Fries, K. (2004). Multicultural teacher education: Research, practice, and policy. In Banks, J. A. (Ed.), *Handbook of research on multicultural education* (2nd ed., pp. 931–975). San Francisco, CA: Jossey-Bass.

Lac, V., & Diamond, J. (2019). Working for racial equity at the margins: Teacher-leaders facilitate a book study on race in a predominantly white suburban high school. *Journal of Cases in Educational Leadership, 22*(2), 54–67.

ADDITIONAL RESOURCES

- Lewis, A. E., & Diamond, J. B. (2015). *Despite the best intentions: How racial inequality thrives in good schools.* Oxford, UK: Oxford University Press.
- Milner, H. R., IV. (2020). *Start where you are, but don't stay there: Understanding diversity, opportunity gaps, and teaching in today's classrooms* (2nd ed.). Cambridge, MA: Harvard Education Press.
- Singleton, G. E. (2014). *Courageous conversations about race: A field guide for achieving equity in schools.* Thousand Oaks, CA: Corwin Press.
- Tatum, B. D. (2017). *Why are all the Black kids sitting together in the cafeteria? And other conversations about race.* New York: Basic Books.

CHAPTER 9

Companion Article: Mission Ready

Globalization, Diversity, and Inclusion Viewed through the Experiences of Children of Military Service Members

Chadrhyn Pedraza

GOAL

The goal of this companion guide's activities is to challenge educational leaders to look for ways to provide a platform for children of military service members (CMSM) to share their experiences, empower them to utilize these experiences to their support learning, and ask educators to identify gaps in research, policy, and practice.

BACKGROUND

CMSM will have moved approximately every three years during their parent(s)' military career (Strobino & Salvaterra, 2000). With each new permanent change of station comes the opportunity to learn about a new culture and community. There is no research on the experiences of CMSM relating to their perspectives on navigating multiple cultural borders. Extant literature has limited its focus on the impact of military-related life events on the population's psychological health (De Pedro et al., 2011). While this scholarship is crucial to understanding the services needed to support CMSM, it confines these students to a single narrative (Adichie, 2009). The activities aim to bring attention to the multifaceted experiences of CMSM and the potential for these experiences to inform research in diversity, inclusion, and globalization.

THEORY TO PRACTICE

John Dewey (1938) called educational leaders to act as sentinels to observe connections between lived experiences and formal learning. As the world grows increasingly interconnected, we must consider how we support integrating life experiences with communities outside of the local with lessons in traditional school disciplines in the humanities, social sciences, math, and physical sciences to present a holistic learning environment for all students. For CMSM, these life experiences may include visits to actual historical sites or exposure to educational systems and curricula vastly different from our own in the United States. It may involve the adoption of international customs and traditions as they develop a culturally hybrid identity. As Massey (1998) pointed out, cultural hybridity incorporates local traditions with global influences to create a new identity representing globalization's effects at multiple levels. Brooks and Normore (2010) referred to this intertwining of the local and global as glocal, arguing for the development of glocal literacies by educational leaders to better prepare students to participate in a globalized society.

ACTIVITIES

1. Olivia is in the eighth grade attending what is now her sixth school on her third continent. At the age of five, her family had been stationed in South Korea. At the time, her mother started homeschooling, but Olivia, outgoing and social by nature, craved more interaction with children her age. The family's only option was the local Korean kindergarten, where the staff did not speak English. Despite the language barrier, Olivia thrived and fully immersed herself in the culture. As a student in your class, you've observed Olivia engage with new students to help them transition to their new environment. Consider the ways you can continue to empower Olivia. Ask yourself the following questions: What were experiences attending the Korean kindergarten? How have these experiences informed the way she approaches new students?

2. You are a researcher interested in CMSM experiences with frequent permanent changes of station. Design a study to explore their views on the process.
   a. Use a qualitative design.
   b. Use a quantitative design.
3. Jacob's family has permanently changed station back to the continental United States after spending three years in the United Kingdom. During the math lesson, he volunteers to complete the problem on the board. As he begins to solve the problem, you notice that Jacob has employed an entirely different process from that which you have been teaching the class.
   a. How would you approach Jacob regarding his methods?
   b. Take a moment to research educational systems around the world to gain insight into different curricula.
4. De Pedro, Esqueda, Cederbaum, and Astor (2014) explored schools' "homegrown" initiatives to support CMSM. Research the programs offered in your community. What are your ideas for efforts in your area?

REFLECTION

- The experiences of CMSM are understudied in the field of education. Take a moment to reflect on your experiences, if any, with military families. How can you use these experiences for research? For practice?
- CMSM are not the only highly mobile population. Which students are considered highly mobile in your schools? Are there support systems designed to aid in their transition? How can you support their learning by utilizing their own experiences and assisting them in finding connections?
- What are your own experiences with navigating new cultures and communities? If you have not left your local community, in what ways can you expand your exposure to global society?

REFERENCES

Adichie, C. (2009). *The danger of a single story* [Video file]. Retrieved from https://www.ted.com/talks/chimamanda_ngozi_adichie_the_danger_of_a_single_story

Brooks, J. S., & Normore, A. H. (2010). Educational leadership and globalization: Literacy for a global perspective. *Educational Policy*, *24*(1), 52–82.

De Pedro, K. M. T., Astor, R. A., Benbenishty, R., Estrada, J., Smith, G. R. D., & Esqueda, M. C. (2011). The children of military service members: Challenges, supports, and future educational research. *Review of Educational Research*, *81*(4), 566–618.

De Pedro, K. T., Esqueda, M. C., Cederbaum, J. A., & Astor, R. A. (2014). District, school, and community stakeholder perspectives on the experiences of military-connected students. *Teachers College Record*, *116*, 1–32.

Dewey, J. (1938). *Experience and education*. New York: Macmillan.

Massey, D. (1998). The spatial construction of youth cultures. In *Cool places* (pp. 132–140). New York: Routledge.

Strobino, J., & Salvaterra, M. (2000). School transitions among adolescent children of military personnel: A strengths perspective. *Children and Schools*, *22*(2), 95–107.

CHAPTER 10

Companion Article: Harlem's Motherwork
A Valuable Resource for Urban School Leaders

Terri Watson

GOAL

The goal of this exercise is to provide urban school leaders with the appropriate tools to inform, reframe, and extend traditional models of parent involvement and to ultimately improve student achievement. Harlem's Motherwork is offered as an exemplar, as it a culturally relevant model of parent involvement that rejects negative stereotypes of families and communities of color held by far too many urban school leaders.

BACKGROUND

In the spring of 1966, James Coleman, a sociologist at Johns Hopkins University, and his colleagues released the "Equality of Educational Opportunity" report. The study, known to many as the Coleman Report, was a mandate of the *Civil Rights Act of 1964* (Pub. L. 88-352, 78 Stat. 241 [1964], hereinafter the Act). The act was intended to protect voting rights and prohibit racial segregation in schools, the workforce, and other public spaces as well as discrimination in employment based on "race, color, religion, sex or national origin." The act also required the commissioner of education to conduct a survey of the nation's public schools within two years in order to investigate the availability of educational opportunities (or lack thereof) based on student race and other demographic characteristics.

The Coleman Report (Coleman et al., 1966) was the first large-scale study of its kind. Findings revealed that America's public schools were "separate and unequal." Black children were found to attend the most segregated schools in the country. In fact, the researchers exposed segregation as both policy and practice in many of the nation's private and public institutions. Segregation is a direct result of racism. Unfortunately, racism is a reality for Black people (Bell, 1980). Despite the fact that Black America has always sought access to a high-quality education (Foster, 1997; Tillman, 2004; Walker, 1996), many teachers and school leaders were found to hold deficit perspectives of Black children and their families (Du Bois, 1935; Woodson, 1933/2005). As a result of this bias, schools located in communities of color tend to utilize traditional models of parent involvement that are normative and reductive (Reynolds, 2010).

THEORY TO PRACTICE

Parent involvement is an essential component of student achievement. The Coleman Report revealed that Black mothers in the metropolitan Northeast section of the United States read to their children before they started school, set high expectations for them, and attended PTA meetings more frequently in comparison to their White counterparts. These findings are best exemplified in the advocacy and efforts of Mae Mallory and the Harlem Nine. The Harlem mothers successfully challenged New York City's "separate and unequal" schools (see *In the Matter of Charlene Skipwith and Another* (13 Misc.2d 325 [1958])). Dubbed the Harlem Nine by local media (Farmer, 2017), the mothers and othermothers demonstrated a culturally relevant model of parent involvement I termed Harlem's Motherwork in an attempt to push back on negative stereotypes of parents and communities of color held by far too many urban school leaders.

ACTIVITIES

Harlem's Motherwork is a valuable resource for urban school leaders. In order to capitalize on the agency of people of color, particularly Black mothers and othermothers, urban school leaders should do the following:

1. Attend and host community-based events to identify and engage the mothers and othermothers.
2. Understand their current motherwork and find ways to make the school and its service providers available and accessible to them.
3. Share school data and partner with community members, including mothers and othermothers, to address systemic inequities that hinder student progress.
4. Celebrate wins, big and small, with the school's community.

REFLECTIONS

As a Harlem native and a scholar-activist, I wanted to celebrate the advocacy and efforts of Harlem's mothers and to exemplify the important relationship between parent involvement and student achievement (Coleman et al., 1966). Importantly, I wanted to provide urban school leaders with the appropriate tools to inform, reframe, and extend traditional models of parent involvement and to ultimately improve student achievement.

REFERENCES

Bell, D. A. (1980). *Brown v. Board of Education and the interest-convergence dilemma. Harvard Law Review, 33*, 1–34.

Coleman, J. S., Campbell, E. Q., Hobson, C. J., McPartland, J., Mood, A. M., Weinfeld, F. D., et al. (1996). *Equality of educational opportunity* (Vols. 1 and 2) (OE-38001; Superintendent of Documents Catalog No. FS 5.238:38001). Washington, DC: U.S. Government Printing Office.

Du Bois, W. E. B. (1935). Does the negro need separate schools? *Journal of Negro Education, 4*(3), 328–355.

Farmer, A. (2017). *Remaking Black power: How Black women transformed an era.* Chapel Hill: University of North Carolina Press.

Foster, M. (1997). *Black teachers on teaching.* New York: New Press.

Reynolds, R. (2010). "They think you're lazy," and other messages Black parents send their Black sons: An exploration of critical race theory in the examination of educational outcomes for Black males. *Journal of African American Males in Education, 1*(1), 144–163.

Tillman, L. C. (2004). African American principals and the legacy of *Brown*. *Review of Research in Education, 28*, 101–146.

Walker, V. S. (1996). *Their highest potential: An African American school community in the segregated South.* Chapel Hill: University of North Carolina Press.

Woodson, C. G. (2005). *The mis-education of the Negro.* Mineola, NY: Dover. (Original work published 1933.)

Part IV

URBAN KNOWLEDGE
AND WAYS OF KNOWING

CHAPTER 11

Companion Article: Critically Conscious Educational Leadership Development through the Use of Pláticas in an Agentic Learning Space

Brenda Rubio, Chris Milk-Bonilla, and Randy Clinton Bell

GOAL

Academia Cuauhtli pláticas are intentionally structured to build relationships among the teachers and facilitate discussions about the social factors that impact their curricular instruction. The ultimate goal is to identify pedagogic actions that can be taken in response to oppressive schooling and social forces that marginalize the cultural and linguistic knowledge of our students, families, educators, and communities and to work toward recentering these alternative epistemologies. Educators are encouraged to take individual and collective action within their traditional schooling spaces and through their work in Academia Cuauhtli.

BACKGROUND

Cuauhtli teachers use the plática space to strengthen their individual practice and build a collaborative practice with their peers. Since teachers are often discouraged or actively prohibited from discussing societal factors on their traditional school campuses, the trust-building component of the pláticas is crucial. They need to feel safe to discuss these issues openly and to help them make sense of their own experiences and feelings toward the topics discussed. These conversations serve as a gateway into more in-depth discussions about their pedagogical beliefs and purpose for seeking out and teaching at Academia Cuauhtli.

THEORY TO PRACTICE

Strategic Planning for Pláticas

The strategic planning for Academia Cuauhtli takes into consideration organizational factors and pedagogical and relational objectives when deciding on the goals for the pláticas. Organizational factors include considerations for the materials and funding that are available or needed to teach a specific lesson plan. Pedagogical objectives include decisions over lesson plans and activities, while the relational objectives center the needs of the educators. Generally, Cuauhtli teachers and program coordinators set the plática goals together based on future objectives set during previous meetings and current events. There are times that conditions in the community or the district changed dramatically from week to week, forcing us to adapt to new realities. Thus, flexibility is essential.

Pedagogical Objectives

Pláticas are guided by the teachers' material realities and what the teachers know about the material realities of their students. Thus, considerations for the schooling context and an understanding of why this context drove them to seek out Academia Cuauhtli is important. This allows us to have a general idea of the material realities of the Cuauhtli teachers. Through guided questions, Cuauhtli teachers talk about the successes and barriers they have faced when teaching a dual-language curriculum that centers their students' and communities' cultural and linguistic knowledge. These successes and barriers typically fall under four categories: society, schooling, curricular issues, and instructional issues.

Relational Objectives

Relationship building with and between teachers facilitates more profound and more complex discussions about issues that are critical to Latinx students and community. Guided by the concept of relationship-based leadership (Richardson & Earle, 2006), we aim to learn about Cuauhtli teachers' internal motivations for teaching at their particular school. We use these discussions to uncover ways to support Cuauthli's vision and create accountability for achieving this vision through our instructional goals. We also aim to acknowledge and support the holistic needs of Cuauhtli teachers themselves, who share similar backgrounds to our students and community members.

ACTIVITIES

Pedagogical Objectives

The following sample questions are used to guide conversations about recent community events and their impact:

A. *Society.* According to your students and families, what impact have recent events had on them? What needs have arisen from these events or been expressed?
B. *School.* What assistance or support is available to you and your students on your campus to meet these needs? Through the district? Through community resources? That can be leveraged by us as a collaborative?
C. *Curricular issues.* In what ways can you integrate discussion or activities about current events into your curriculum? What readings or supplemental materials can we draw from or create to build a lesson plan aligned with district and state standards?
D. *Instructional issues.* How did your students respond to these lessons? In what ways can these lesson plans be improved?

Relational Objectives

The following sample questions and activities used to build relationships during pláticas among Academia Cuauhtli educators:

A. *Building trust.* What inspired you to become a bilingual education teacher? What continues to inspire you in the classroom? Draw a picture that illustrates the main values that guide your teaching.
B. *Discussing divisive issues.* What is our personal vision for Academia Cuauhtli? What is the overlap in our visions? How do we

express this vision separately? What priorities and actions do we need to set based on these?

REFERENCE

Richardson, C., & Earle, K. (2006). *Relationship based leadership*. Lanham, MD: University Press of America.

CHAPTER 12

Companion Article: HQPE

Exploring the Role of Physical Education in Facing America's Educational Debt

Samuel R. Hodge, Martha James-Hassan, and Alexander Vigo-Valentín

GOAL

The purpose of the exercises contained in this component of the Companion Guide is to support a better understanding of historical and cultural barriers to engagement in physical activity (PA) and to support efforts to increase access to and participation in high-quality physical education (HQPE) and PA for all, particularly historically and often contemporarily marginalized (e.g., Black and Latinx) students.

BACKGROUND

For some 60 years now, the benefits of physical activity have been well established. For example, Hein and Ryan (1960) articulated the importance of physical activity in their article "The Contributions of Physical Activity to Human Well-Being." Since the 1970s (and true today as well), school physical education programs have explored curricular innovations and instructional practices to align with the knowledge and needs of the times. The goal of HQPE is the development of *physical literacy*. Physical literacy, as defined by the Society of Health and Physical Educators of America (commonly known as SHAPE America), is the ability to move with confidence and competence in a wide variety of environments for the benefit of the whole person (SHAPE America, n.d.). HQPE is, therefore, a medium for guiding students in the process of developing the skills, knowledge, and habits to live a well-balanced healthy and physically active life. Accordingly, educators and scholars have articulated various benefits of HQPE programs, such as providing regular opportunities for students to (1) learn and practice movement and sport skills in active and dynamic environments; (2) learn and practice appropriate social skills and ethical behaviors; (3) interact with peers from ethnically, culturally, economically, and linguistically diverse backgrounds; (4) participate in health-related physical activities; and (5) develop meaningful and lasting relationships with others while demonstrating self-responsibility and social responsibility. In fact, as pre-K–12 schools focus more and more on the social and emotional learning needs of students (Weissberg & Cascarino, 2013), it is critical to point out that mental and social health aspects along with physical health are of great benefit to all students working and learning together in integrated general HQPE programs.

Barriers to participation in HQPE range from declining school budgets and an academic focus exclusively on alpha and numeric literacy to societal misconceptions, cultural misalignment, and individual resistance. The result of this range of barriers collectively manifests in the fact that too often Black and Latinx students have little or no access to adequate learning experiences in encore content areas, including physical education (Kraehe, Acuff, & Travis, 2016).

In addition to advocacy for ample educational funding and dissemination of research on the benefits of a well-rounded curriculum to inform policies and practices, the promotion of cultural fluency is essential to the kind of course correction that is necessary to ensure that each student in every school across the United States has access to HQPE. Physical education teachers who are culturally fluent should demonstrate both knowledge and skill at identifying issues, addressing problems, reflecting, and thinking critically about what cultural competency and relevance mean in teaching historically marginalized, minoritized students (Hodge & James-Hassan, 2014) with the understanding that they will need to address sociocultural and historical biases that marginalize physical activity and physical education. The expectation of cultural fluency is that educators must be able to effectively function in dynamic multicultural and linguistically diverse environments in which cultural differences are embraced without assigning values (e.g., good or bad) to such differences to interrupt inequitable access to PA and HQPE.

THEORY TO PRACTICE

In addressing the educational debt that is the result of the historical and present-day marginalization of Black and Latinx students in public education in the United States as it specifically applies to physical education, it is essential to identify and promote essential components and best practices of HQPE, as well as to identify potential psychosocial, historical, and cultural barriers to individual and group participation in HQPE and PA. Theoretical models for consideration in this task include critical race theory, critical pedagogy, cultural fluency, and culturally relevant pedagogies.

ACTIVITIES

Exercise 1: Identifying Hegemonic Reproduction through the Hidden Curriculum

Consider rituals, routines, content, curriculum, and instructional strategies based on the components of quality physical education programs illustrated in table 12.1 to generate a list of five or six common practices that you use or have seen used in physical education classes. What are the intended outcomes of each of those practices? What other lessons might students learn from engaging in those practices?

Example: *Squads* or *squad lines* are often used as an organizational strategy in the beginning of physical education lessons. Squads and squad lines in this instance are forward-facing lines of students—usually seated—for attendance and/or instruction. (Component #4: Teaches management and self-discipline)

1. The intended outcomes are that it speeds up the process of taking attendance because teachers can see a gap where an absent student should be, and it serves as a simple way to divide the class into groups or teams for physical activity.
2. Possible unintended consequences are that it undermines community building by organizing students in a fashion that does not readily allow engagement, and it forces students to face the back of students' heads. Further, it does not promote the development

of self-regulation or diverse interactions, thereby signaling to students that these learning areas are not important.

Table 12.1. Components of a Quality Physical Education (PE) Program

Component	
1.	Is organized around content standards that offer direction and continuity to instruction and evaluation
2.	Is student centered and based on the developmental urges, cultures, tendencies, and interests of students
3.	Has physical activity and motor skill development at its core
4.	Teaches management skills and self-discipline
5.	Emphasizes inclusion of all students
6.	Emphasizes instruction focused on the process of learning rather than performance outcomes
7.	Teaches lifetime activities that students can use to promote their health and personal values
8.	Teaches cooperative and responsibility skills and helps students develop sensitivity to multiple diversities

Source: Hodge, Lieberman, and Murata (2012, p. 20)

Exercise 2: Applying an Equity Lens

Generate a list of real-world policy or practice decisions that could be common in pre-K–12 physical education. This could include a range of topics from what content to use to address a standard, to master scheduling, to engaging with parents, or to developing a system-wide wellness policy or assessment plan. Then use the equity lens below to engage colleagues in critical discussions of the problems of practice that emerge and how to mitigate negative consequences for the students and communities served.

Equity Decision-Making Lens: Questions to Consider for any Policy, Program, Practice, Decision, or Action (Maryland Association of Boards of Education, 2020)

1. Who are the underrepresented groups affected by this policy, program, practice, decision, or action? What are the potential impacts on (individuals in) these groups?
2. Does this policy, program, practice, decision, or action worsen existing disparities or produce other unintended consequences?

3. How have you intentionally involved stakeholders who are also members of the communities affected by this policy, program, practice, decision, or action? Can you validate your assessments in items 1 and 2, having considered this stakeholder reaction?
4. What are barriers to more equitable outcomes (e.g., mandated, political, emotional, financial, programmatic, or managerial)?
5. How will you (a) mitigate the negative impacts be mitigated and (b) address the barriers identified above?

REFLECTION

Physical education in pre-K–12 education is far too often seen as being an add-on or extra. This is evidenced by the frequency with which physical educators are referred to by the room in which they teach as *gym teachers* or as *resource, special, support, extracurricular*, or *prep-time* teachers. This second-class lens on physical education can lead to overlooking the academic, social, emotional, and physical benefits of engaging in meaningful, joyous, and developmentally appropriate movement experiences. Further, even as curriculum models are developed and employed to modernize physical education, rarely is consideration given to examining the hidden curriculum or the sociopolitical context of the school community. Considering the intended and unintended consequences and outcomes of decisions in advance through an equity lens allows us to introduce the idea of Universal Design for Equity (UDE). The idea of UDE is formulated around the central concepts of Universal Design for Learning (UDL) (Story, Mueller, & Mace, 1998) and applies those concepts to addressing the needs of historically oppressed learners, newcomers, and traditionally accommodated students. As conceptualized in UDE, use of UDL assumes that the barriers to learning are in the design of the experience, not the learner (Posey, n.d.). Further, implementing a perspective of UDE requires those who design curricula, deliver instruction, and assess learning to reflect on the goals of a learning experience to ensure that it provides an appropriate challenge for each student; that materials have a flexible format and support an expansive definition of text allowing multiple representations of content to support each students' learning; that methods are promoted that are flexible and diverse enough to provide appropriate learning experiences, challenges, and supports for each student; and that assessments are sufficiently flexible to provide accurate, ongoing information that helps teachers adjust instruction and maximize learning (Hitchcock, Meyer, Rose, & Jackson, 2002). Transforming physical education through policies and practices that are intentionally invested in ensuring equity in access and culturally responsive and sustainable curriculum and instruction represents the hope in HQPE to increase participation and positive experiences in physical education and thereby support physical activity and wellness in underrepresented communities.

REFERENCES

Hein, F. V., & Ryan, A. J. (1960). The contributions of physical activity to physical health. *Research Quarterly, 31*(2), 263–285.

Hitchcock, C., Meyer, A., Rose, D. & Jackson, R. (2002, November/December). Providing new access to the general curriculum: Universal Design for Learning. *Teaching Exceptional Children*, 8–17. https://journals.sagepub.com/doi/pdf/10.1177/004005990203500201?casa_token=An4-tPzePNwAAAAA:M1hRqD9eF8Tvv3r-I45PoQaUndkHIpZWD6DB_SN1pgH0lh2EKoyBDxMk-nQa13vftaVAcFTg4ohvBg.

Hodge, S. R., & James-Hassan, M. (2014). African American males and physical education. In Moore, J. L., III, & Lewis, C. L. (Eds.), *African American male students in PreK-12 schools: Informing research, policy, and practice* (Vol. 2, pp. 305–344). Bingley: Emerald Group Publishing.

Hodge, S. R., Lieberman, L. J., & Murata, N. M. (2012). *Essentials of teaching adapted physical education: Diversity, culture, and inclusion*. New York: Taylor & Francis.

Kraehe, A. M., Acuff, J. B., & Travis, S. (2016). Equity, the arts, and urban education: A review. *Urban Review, 48*(2), 220–244. https://doi.org/10.1007/s11256-016-0352-2.

Maryland Association of Boards of Education. (2020). *Equity lens*. Annapolis, MD: Maryland Association of Boards of Education. https://www.mabe.org/about/equity-initiatives.

Posey, A. (n.d.). *Universal Design for Learning (UDL): A teacher's guide*. New York: CAST, Inc. https://www.understood.org/en/school-learning/for-educators/universal-design-for learning/understanding-universal

-design-for-learning?gclid=EAIaIQobChMImOvU05r-5wIVhYCfCh28wQ_2EAAYASAAEgIjXvD_BwE.

Society of Health and Physical Educators. (n.d.). *Physical literacy.* https://www.shapeamerica.org/events/physicalliteracy.aspx?hkey=61893e49-8a9e-430c-b4f5-8267480cb421.

Story, M. F., Mueller, J. L., & Mace, R. L. (1998). *The universal design file: Designing for people of all ages and abilities.* https://files.eric.ed.gov/fulltext/ED460554.pdf.

Weissberg, R. P., & Cascarino, J. (2013). Academic learning + social-emotional learning = national priority. *Phi Delta Kappan, 95*(2), 8–13. https://doi.org/10.1177/003172171309500203.

CHAPTER 13

Companion Article: Women's Perspectives on Deconstructing the Urban Ivory Tower for Black Women Faculty

Risha Berry, Tomika Ferguson, and Whitney Sherman Newcomb

GOAL

The purpose of this exercise is to help readers learn more about the structural barriers to retention for Black women faculty (teaching and tenure track) at predominantly White institutions. Revealing structural barriers to the retention of Black women faculty through bricolage narratives offers a novel approach to naming structural barriers and critical incidents that systematically restrict the retention of Black women faculty. These barriers are systematically constructed and ultimately lead to "justified" dichotomous rationales (meeting or not meeting annual performance outcomes) for Black women faculty that effectively promote their push-out. Specifically, we offer department chairs a tool for reflection while moving through the phases of preparing, recruiting, and retaining/promoting Black women faculty in their departments. This activity pushes chairs beyond purported self beliefs and engages them in reflecting on whether their beliefs are enacted on a regular basis.

BACKGROUND

Faculty diversity can foster inclusive learning environments (National Center for Educational Statistics [NCES], 2019). In the fall of 2017, only 6 percent of faculty members at two- and four-year institutions were Black (NCES, 2018). The lack of presence of Black faculty in higher education limits diverse perspectives in how we think holistically about promoting equity in educational leadership contexts.

Conversely, the presence of Black faculty supports success for a wider range of students. In the fall of 2017, the NCES (2018) reported that there were a total of 821,168 full-time faculty in degree-granting postsecondary institutions. Approximately 18 percent, or 45,427, were Black. Of the 45,427 Black faculty, only 57 percent were women. In short, 3 percent of all full-time faculty in higher education were Black women (NCES, 2018).

Low numbers of Black women faculty, in particular, illuminate a challenge. Increasing the number of Black women faculty is difficult without institutional commitment. For example, when Black women faculty have minimal integration into their academic environments, they may risk facing fewer opportunities for research (Turner, 2002). In a publish-or-perish environment, faculty of color at institutions where there are fewer opportunities for research are at a disadvantage for tenure and promotion (Turner, González, & Wood, 2008). The opportunity for higher-education institutions to increase sustainable practices for the recruitment and retention of Black women faculty is important. It is therefore imperative that we draw attention to the experiences of Black women faculty within educational leadership departments who often lead the charge and instruction of equity-focused work within their departments. Their retention and success is critical to the production of equity-minded practitioners in our diverse schools.

THEORY TO PRACTICE

Narratives that discuss the barriers that Black women encounter as faculty members detail individual and shared experiences as they transverse through the academy. The road map from recruitment to retention of Black women faculty members includes three phases: preparation, recruitment, and retention/promotion. Often, Black women are met with structural barriers that are inherent to the academy but do not consider the influence of their identities and agency in light of how institutional policies and practices are culpable in promoting or restricting their retention. Narratives serve as powerful road maps identifying structural barriers. They play key roles in decoding the ivory tower by identifying how structural barriers are created and implemented in the academy. Narratives also provide liberation in naming critical incidents and provide new strategies to decode invisible barriers for the successful promotion and retention of Black women faculty, and they serve as road maps for department chairs by revealing critical incidents through the identification of new pathways for institutional change. Department chairs can have power and agency that enhance the experiences of Black women faculty. The combined use of Black women faculty narratives and reflection by department chairs can lead to positive change for Black women faculty.

The activity below is designed to promote equitable practices to support Black women faculty members. Through critical self-reflection by department chairs, there is an opportunity to reflect over barriers that Black women faculty may face and to identify strategies that are based on individual ability, personal growth, and institutional opportunities to promote equitable practices within their departments.

ACTIVITY: EQUITABLE PRACTICES TO SUPPORT BLACK WOMEN FACULTY MEMBERS

Department Chair Reflection

Phase 1: Preparation, Structural Barrier: Mentorship

Reflection Questions
- In what ways have I provided opportunities for Black women graduate students and faculty in my department to have access to and identify relevant mentors aligned with their research and professional interests?
- What are the professional and academic goals of the Black women in my department?
- In what ways can I advocate (use of power, privilege, and agency) for Black women in my department to define their research agenda and identify opportunities to meet their goals?

For Further Consideration
- Adequate preparation for a career in the academy takes strategic planning. Some students enter the PhD program directly from the master's degree, some return after a short (or long) hiatus, while

others return to gain more skills to enhance their current career or are interested in a career switch to the academy. Each of these conditions is unique. If students enter full-time, they may have the opportunity to serve as a graduate assistant. These assistantships, in theory, are designed to support students in learning the ropes of the academy through experiential learning in research, teaching, and service. However, these experiences may vary according to many factors.
- Contrary to popular belief, one mentor will not meet the array of needs of a student or a new faculty member. A faculty member needs several mentors in a variety of spaces (Gayles, 2019) to provide the following:
  - Substantive feedback (department colleagues, professional editor, readers—intellectual community);
  - Sponsorships (senior faculty in department)
  - Access to opportunities (on-campus mentors, off-campus mentors, peer mentors)
  - Accountability for what really matters
  - Safe spaces
  - Intellectual community (readers at different levels: 0 to 25 percent done, 25 to 50 percent done, 50 to 75 percent done, 75 to 100 percent done)
  - Role models
  - Emotional support (friends, family, other)
  - Professional development (on campus, off campus)

Phase 2: Recruitment, Structural Barrier: Hiring

Reflection Questions
- How have I articulated and scrutinized my beliefs about inclusion and equity that may be embedded in department decisions and behaviors?
- Have I led discussions with my department that consider how specific beliefs about race, ethnicity, and gender may influence the candidate pool, needs of the department, and potential support for a new faculty member?

- In what ways is my department prepared to recruit, support, and retain Black women faculty members? Have I led the creation of a department culture that is inclusive, welcoming, and safe? Do department policies support this?

For Further Consideration
- Tenure-track faculty positions are limited and highly competitive. The candidate pool may include assistant professors who are interested in transitioning to a new university and have had experience with the academy through teaching, research, and service. It may also include recent graduates who have had strong graduate assistantship postdoctoral experiences. And the pool might often include more veteran graduates with demonstrated experiences through their careers but less experience with teaching and publication.

Phase 3: Retention and Promotion, Structural: Advocacy

Reflection Questions
- Have I examined all forms of evaluation and assessment of faculty members in my department? What is the importance and influence of race, ethnicity, and gender in annual evaluations and promotion and tenure processes?
- In what ways are identified barriers (e.g., service load, institutional expectations, teaching responsibilities) known and addressed for Black women faculty members?
- What are the limitations and opportunities of my role to influence and create policies to promote the visibility of Black women in my university?

For Further Consideration
- Shared governance is an effective tool used to develop and implement inclusive policies and practices that affect the entire faculty community.
- Inclusion should be a school-wide responsibility, not solely a department chair responsibility.

REFLECTION

Academia is sustained on norms that are not traditionally inclusive of Black women faculty members. This is evidenced by the small number of full-time Black women in the academy at all levels. Although norms are not often inclusive of Black women faculty, they are held to the same standards as their White peers. In order to create more equitable practices for them, the experiences of Black women faculty must be placed within a raced and gendered context for their success in the academy. Research has demonstrated marginalization for Black women, including being hypervisible and invisible in academic spaces, being silenced or ignored, having their research agendas critiqued as not scholarly (Smith, 1999), and being overloaded with service but not valued for their contributions to student success and teaching (Kelly, Williams, & Gayles, 2017). For them to be retained and promoted, opportunities of support must be equitable and aligned with expectations within the academy.

Identifying structural barriers to the promotion and retention for Black women faculty through narrative and reflection aids in the design and early identification of structural signifiers of inequities and offers new insight into accountability mechanisms for predominantly White institutions to prepare, recruit, and retain Black women faculty. The activity offered here is not exhaustive but is designed to be an impetus for reflection for department chairs leading change efforts.

REFERENCES

Gayles, J. G. (2019). Re-thinking mentoring: An alternative framework for mentoring pre and post-tenure faculty [PowerPoint slides]. https://ncfdd-production-file-uploads.s3.amazonaws.com/media%2Fd1e%2FRethinking+Mentoring+%28Half+Day%29.pdf.

Kelly, B. T., Williams, C. D., & Gayles, J. G. (2017). Recruitment without retention: A critical case of black faculty unrest. *Journal of Negro Education, 86*(3), 305–317. https://doi.org/10.7709/jnegroeducation.86.3.0305.

National Center for Education Statistics (NCES). (2018). *Digest of education statistics.* https://nces.ed.gov/programs/digest/d18/tables/dt18_315.20.asp.

National Center for Education Statistics (NCES). (2019). *The condition of education 2019* (NCES 2019-144). https://https://nces.ed.gov/fastfacts/display.asp?id=61.

Smith, P. J. (1999). Failing to mentor Sapphire: The actionability of blocking Black women from initiating mentoring relationships. *UCLA Women's Law Journal, 10,* 120–130.

Turner, C. S. V. (2002). Women of color in academe: Living with multiple marginality. *Journal of Higher Education, 73,* 74–93.

Turner, C. S. V., González, J. C., & Wood, J. L. (2008). Faculty of color in academe: What 20 years of literature tells us. *Journal of Diversity in Higher Education, 1*(3), 139–168. https://doi.org/10.1037/a0012837.

Part V

URBAN POLITICS AND EDUCATIONAL LEADERSHIP

CHAPTER 14

Companion Article: Urban Education and Educational Leadership Graduate Preparation Programs

Preparing Graduate Students Coming from and Going into Urban Pre-K–12 Settings

René O. Guillaume and Elizabeth C. Apodaca

GOAL

The goal of this exercise is to explore ways in which educational leadership preparation programs can support their graduate students coming from urban environments while readying them to be impactful leaders under conditions demonstrated in urban schools. Educational leadership programs will be better suited for graduate students who have attended urban pre-K–12 schools if they address the unique qualities urban schools operate under. By offering a culturally responsive curriculum, these programs can ensure that their students are well served and prepared to lead in a twenty-first-century educational setting.

BACKGROUND

Almost one-third of all U.S. students enrolled in pre-K–12 schools live in urban settings (U.S. Department of Education, 2019). The issue of urban-educated students not being adequately prepared for college has been a talking point in the United States for decades (Dwarte & Anderson, 2016; Roderick, Nagaoka, & Coca, 2009; Savitz, 2012). Although federal legislation focused on school reform has had some positive impact, urban-educated students continue to lag in college preparedness and college access.

Educational leadership preparation programs have a unique reach in that they not only work with students coming from urban educational settings but also graduate students who will be moving into leadership positions in urban schools. Because of this, it's imperative that they offer a culturally responsive curriculum that offers graduate students a deep understanding of urban education at the pre-K–12 level. To be as impactful as possible, these programs must be redesigned to support both students coming from urban environments and graduates moving into urban educational workforce leadership.

THEORY TO PRACTICE

To assist graduate students from urban pre-K–12 settings in becoming future educational leaders, a deep understanding of the issues related to urban education must be embedded in the curriculum of educational leadership graduate programs. However, it is not sufficient to focus on understanding; these students must also be taught how to create reform.

The following activities focus on building a strong understanding of the impact that urban education has on individuals and institutions. They aim at furthering the conversation by asking the reader to consider ways in which educational leadership programs can be modified to better support urban-educated students. Using a theory of change approach (Connell & Klem, 2000), the reader is asked to begin developing a plan for reform in the curriculum and programming within a department of educational leadership.

ACTIVITIES

1. Examine the curriculum and program goals of an educational leadership graduate program specializing in urban education advocacy:
    a. Identify the courses in which urban educational issues are addressed.
    b. Look for evidence of ways in which the curriculum and learning objectives of individual courses align and build on each other throughout the program.
    c. Compare the findings to what is going on at your institution.
    d. Suggest ways they could be added to or replace what the institution is currently offering.

2. Research public policy or legislation related to pre-K–12 urban education:
   a. Identify current policy on urban education in a state of your choice.
   b. Pay attention to the main talking points of the policy.
   c. Identify one (or more) missing or unexamined issue that may impact its effectiveness for students.
   d. Determine some ways in which educational leadership programs could prepare their graduate students for addressing these issues as they transition into school leadership roles.
3. Interview current undergraduate students from urban pre-K–12 settings:
   a. Identify students in your program who were educated in urban U.S. schools.
   b. Focus on their high school experiences with college readiness and college preparation. Ask them to speak to inconsistencies in the programming they received compared to what they found they needed to be successful in college.
   c. Problematize policy and processes that school leaders—in both pre-K–12 and postsecondary settings—could implement at the site level that would better support them.

REFLECTION

It's an expectation that students who complete high school are ready for postsecondary education, but often they arrive at college campuses underprepared academically and with little understanding of how to navigate the environment. Although many urban high schools offer college preparation programs, there seems to be a disconnect between the preparation that students receive there and the expectations that colleges and universities have for their incoming students. This issue is systemic and is not unique to urban schools; however, with almost one-third of all U.S. students enrolled in urban schools (U.S. Department of Education, 2019), it's a problem that we cannot avoid addressing.

When processes are not working, the blame often falls on the participant; this is no different for students educated in urban school settings who are not successful in college. However, this deficit-focused approach of blaming students for their shortcomings does nothing to address the issue. Theory of change is premised on the idea that it is possible to create systemic change through planning (Connell & Klem, 2000). Part of this plan is to look at making changes in the most impactful way in places that have the most influence. We propose that one place is at the postsecondary setting in departments of educational leadership and administration. It is through the implementation of culturally responsive programming that departments of educational leadership have influence on both the students who have graduated from pre-K–12 urban schools and the administrators leading those schools in the future, supporting a pre-K–20 educational focus.

REFERENCES

Connell, J. P., & Klem, A. M. (2000). You can get there from here: Using a theory of change approach to plan urban education reform. *Journal of Educational and Psychological Consultation, 11*(1), 93–120.

Dwarte, M., & Anderson, C. (2016). How to improve college readiness at urban schools: A three-pillared plan is helping low-income students become college and career ready. *Principal Leadership, 16*(6), 36–40.

Roderick, M., Nagaoka, J., & Coca, V. (2009). College readiness for all: The challenge for urban high schools. *Future of Children, 19*(1), 185–210.

Savitz, R. M. (2012). The gap between influence and efficacy: College readiness training, urban school counselors, and the promotion of equity. *Counselor Education and Supervision, 51*(2), 98–111.

U.S. Department of Education, Institute of Education Sciences, National Center for Education Statistics. (2019). *Fast facts: Back to school statistics*. https://nces.ed.gov/fastfacts/display.asp?id=372#PK12_enrollment.

CHAPTER 15

Companion Article: Queering Urban Elementary Schools

Campus Leaders as Allies of Intersectionality

Leanna Lucero and Angela V. E. Owens

GOAL

The purpose of this companion guide is to provide opportunities for educational leaders to engage in activities that move them from learning about research and statistics to actively examining their personal biases and their current campus inclusivity and to create an action plan for implementing changes to create an environment that represents all students and their families.

BACKGROUND

Progress in creating safe U.S. schools for queer youth has slowed or ceased since 2017 (Kosciw, Greytak, Zongrone, Clark, & Truong, 2018). Results from the 2017 National School Climate Survey provide evidence that the majority of queer teens experience bullying or assault on a regular basis at school because of their identity (Kosciw et al., 2018). Results from the same survey revealed several alarming statistics about the school experiences of queer youth: (1) nearly 90 percent of students are assaulted or harassed based on their sexual orientation, perceived sexual orientation, gender, gender expression, race and ethnicity, and/or disability; (2) more than 70 percent of queer students experienced verbal harassment at school based on sexual orientation; and (3) more than 60 percent who reported the harassment said that nothing was done to address the discriminatory remarks, or students were told to ignore the abuse. These alarming statistics are the reason that more than one-third of queer students miss school each year. Additionally, hostile environments such as these negatively affect queer students' educational outcomes and mental health (Kosciw et al., 2018). Queering urban campuses will help to provide and protect every student's human and civil right to a quality public education in a safe environment where no students fear for their safety or right to be who they are.

THEORY TO PRACTICE

Queer theory seeks to disrupt binaries and rethink current practices (Butler, 2004; Robinson, 2005). Using queer theory as a framework provides a foundation for educational leaders to examine their current campus and begin to create a campus improvement plan that includes rethinking campus policies and practices rooted in heteronormativity. Queering urban elementary campuses is a fluid and continuous process that seeks to create inclusivity for all students.

ACTIVITIES

Role-Playing Activities

Identity is socially constructed (e.g., Butler, 2004); therefore, in order to improve outcomes for learners who are in the LGBTQ+ community, purposeful professional development via social interactions needs to occur where leaders and staff can learn how to confront their biases. A technique we recommend is role-playing with the intention of acting out and thinking through biases (Cahnmann-Taylor & Souto-Manning, 2010), thereby challenging the status quo of heterosexual structures. Role play followed by honest discussions is a tool that can be used to queer elementary campuses. We invite you to use the two role-playing activities below to refine your role as a campus administrator in supporting queer youth and their families:

1. Create a speech to deliver to the school community about your stance in supporting queer students and families in your school through professional development, curriculum, family nights, and so on. In your speech, include references to statistics and schol-

arly literature. Address areas in which you anticipate resistance, such as questions from community members, including conservative community organizations, support staff, teachers, fellow administrators, families, and school board members. Practice delivering your speech to a group of supportive colleagues and then ask for feedback to refine your speech. This will provide a good background to rely on when confronted with resistance from the school community.
2. As a campus administrator, you are walking by the teacher workroom. You hear a group of teachers having a conversation that does not support your campus inclusivity policy. They are using anti-queer slurs—"That's so gay," "She is such a little dyke," and "So which bathroom does the tranny use now?" You cannot ignore this behavior and must do something other than ignore it or close the door. Practice what you will say to these teachers, what you will do to follow up, and what actions you will take to address their biases. (If more people are available, then they can role-play the part of the teachers.)

Using Assessments to Create Action Plans for Campus Improvement

Assessing your personal biases and then the campus environment is the first step in determining your campus strengths and areas for improvement. Use the following tools to identify where your campus excels and where it can improve and to create an action plan for creating inclusivity:

1. Complete GLSEN's Personal and School Assessment (found in "Additional Resources") to identify campus strengths and areas for growth in creating a safe and affirming environment for all students. On completion of the assessment, a step-by-step guide is provided to facilitate the design of a plan to create and implement changes within the campus.
2. Download and review the Human Rights Campaign's checklist (found in "Additional Resources") for creating a welcoming LGBTQ- and gender-inclusive school environment. Identify the areas in which your campus excels in creating an inclusive

environment. Then provide examples of how you create the environment for the specific indicator. For example, *Our campus offers a family dance rather than a father–daughter dance. Doing this recognized different family structures rather than heteronormative and traditional family structures.* Finally, create an action plan for areas that need improvement at your campus. Include the steps you need to take, the people involved, the time frame, the training needed, any cost, and how you will follow up on the progress of your action plan.

REFLECTION

Before role-playing and using assessment, what was your view about preparing to address the public about the relevance of integrating these topics into the campus? What confirmed your view? What are some ways your view changed after completing the activities? What tensions do you still have? What will you do to combat your tensions?

REFERENCES

Butler, J. (2004). *Undoing gender.* New York: Routledge.

Cahnmann-Taylor, M., & Souto-Manning, M. (2010). *Teachers act up! Creating multicultural communities through theater.* New York: Teachers College Press.

Kosciw, J. G., Greytak, E. A., Zongrone, A. D., Clark, C. M., & Truong, N. L. (2018). *The 2017 National School Climate Survey: The experiences of lesbian, gay, bisexual, transgender, and queer youth in our nation's schools.* New York: GLSEN.

Robinson, K. (2005). "Queerying" gender: Heteronormativity in early childhood education. *Australian Journal of Early Childhood, 30*(2), 19–28.

ADDITIONAL RESOURCES

- Gay, Lesbian and Straight Education Network Personal and School Assessment

http://nyssca.org/wp-content/uploads/2012/09/GLSENAssessments-and-Next-Steps-Worksheet.pdf
- Human Rights Campaign Checklist for Creating a Welcoming LGBTQ- and Gender-Inclusive School Environment
  http://www.welcomingschools.org/pages/checklist-for-a-welcoming-and-inclusive-school-environment
- Understanding Bullying Behaviors: What Educators Should Know and Can Do
  https://www.aft.org/ae/winter2016-2017/englander
- GLSEN: Ready, Set, Respect Toolkit for Educators
  https://www.glsen.org/sites/default/files/GLSEN%20Ready%20Set%20Respect.pdf
- GLSEN: LGBTQ—Visibility and Integration in Elementary Schools
  https://www.glsen.org/sites/default/files/2019-12/GLSEN_LGBTQ_Integration_Elementary_Resource_2019_1.pdf
- GLSEN: Role Play Activities and Discussion for Teachers and Students
  https://www.glsen.org/activity/instant-replay
- Robinson, K. H., & Ferfolja, T. (2001). "What are we doing this for?" Dealing with lesbian and gay issues in teacher education. *British Journal of Sociology of Education, 22*(1), 121–133.
- Ryan, C. L., & Hermann-Wilmarth, J. (2013). Already on the shelf: Queer readings of award-winning children's literature. *Journal of Literacy Research, 45* (2), 142–172.
- Ryan, C. L., & Hermann-Wilmarth, J. (2018). *Reading the rainbow: LGBTQ-inclusive literacy instruction in the elementary classroom.* New York: Teachers College Press.

CHAPTER 16

Companion Article: Urban School Administrators' Incorporation of Student Voice/Culture and Community Involvement toward School Discipline in Middle Schools

John A. Williams III and Chance W. Lewis

GOAL

This section aims to provide different approaches that assistant principals and principals can use to reduce in-school and out-of-school suspensions for African American and Latinx students. Through providing alternative responses to promote prosocial student behaviors, we intend to bolster practitioners' capability to provide student-centered practices to prevent misbehavior rather than to punitively react to it.

BACKGROUND

Millions of African American and Latinx students are removed from K–12 schooling environments each year in the United States, often for exhibiting behaviors no different than their White peers (U.S. Department of Education, 2018). Research has articulated that the discipline gap (the difference in school discipline rates between White students, African American students, and Latinx students) continues to highlight the stark reality that students of color are treated differently by practitioners, culminating in a disproportionate number of expulsions, in-school and out-of-school suspensions, referrals to law enforcement, and office referrals (Irby, 2014; Kennedy, Murphy, & Jordan, 2017; Richardson, Williams, & Lewis, 2019). Assistant principals and principals are the administrative personnel who finalize all disciplinary recommendations that require a student to be removed from the classroom or the school for a day or more. Research has expounded on two main points about these two positions concerning school discipline: (1) assistant principals are the primary overseer of most student misbehaviors that warrant out-of-class time (Glanz, 1994), and (2) a principal's disciplinary philosophy (restorative or authoritarian) determines how frequently school staff use punitive or alternative discipline options (Skiba et al., 2011).

THEORY TO PRACTICE

Culturally responsive school leadership denotes that educational leaders (i.e., assistant principals and principals) must develop a sociopolitical consciousness that actively seeks to form mutually beneficial relationships between their school and multicultural communities that their students come from and purposefully lead and support educational change that promotes the academic, social, and emotional growth of the students they serve (Khalifa, Gooden, & Davis, 2016). As it relates to school discipline and engaging students in such a manner to increase their learning opportunities in the classroom, assistant principals and principals each have different opportunities to decrease the use of punitive sanctions.

ACTIVITIES

1. Principals should conduct social need surveys with families and organizations in the community to ascertain which community programs are serving the needs of the students now and determine how these programs can be used as behavior support mechanisms.
2. Assistant principals can engage students to determine what alternative discipline options they think would help curtail student misbehavior and improve on the cultural competency, classroom management, and intercultural communication of school staff members.
3. Identify parents and community members who can become part of an interdisciplinary school discipline accountability council that would meet biweekly (or as needed for more severe events)

to review school discipline data, policy, and student disciplinary outcome appeals to ensure transparency and accountability and that the needs of the students are being adhered to when disciplinary recommendations are being made.

REFLECTION

A common myth is that students of color and the communities they come from do not value education, and when educators uphold this belief, they prevent themselves from searching for alternative measures to reform their own behaviors or improve school discipline policies. In reviewing the activities listed, has your relationship or the relationship of your school changed to better support African American and Latinx students? What did you learn about your students that can be used as an asset in implementing restorative practices? Which community organizations are willing to assist the students and staff in your building?

African American and Latinx students require affirming interactions with assistant principals and principals and engaging relationships with community support programs that affirm their social, emotional, and cultural assets. By developing stronger intercultural relationships with African American students and revisiting the list of programs in the community, assistant principals and principals can implement policies, procedures, and practices that draw students in rather than push students out of K–12 schools.

REFERENCES

Glanz, J. (1994). Dilemmas of assistant principals in their supervisory role: Reflections of an assistant principal. *Journal of School Leadership*, *4*(5), 577–590.

Irby, D. J. (2014). Trouble at school: Understanding school discipline systems as nets of social control. *Equity and Excellence in Education*, *47*(4), 513–530.

Kennedy, B. L., Murphy, A. S., & Jordan, A. (2017). Title I middle school administrators' beliefs and choices about using corporal punishment and exclusionary discipline. *American Journal of Education*, *123*(2), 243–279.

Khalifa, M. A., Gooden, M. A., & Davis, J. E. (2016). Culturally responsive school leadership: A synthesis of the literature. *Review of Educational Research, 86*(4), 1272–1311.

Richardson, S. C., Williams, J. A., III, & Lewis, C. W. (2019). Social workers and urban school discipline: Do we need a time out? *Urban Social Work, 3*(2), 207–230. doi:10.1891/2474-8684.3.2.207.

Skiba, R. J., Horner, R. H., Chung, C. G., Rausch, M. K., May, S. L., & Tobin, T. (2011). Race is not neutral: A national investigation of African American and Latino disproportionality in school discipline. *School Psychology Review, 40*(1), 85–107.

U.S. Department of Education. (2018). *2015–2016 Office of Civil Rights data collection: School climate and safety.* https://www2.ed.gov/about/offices/list/ocr/docs/school-climate-and-safety.pdf.

ADDITIONAL RESOURCES

- California Guide to Fixing School Discipline
    http://njpsa.org/documents/pdf/FixSchoolDiscipline.pdf
- School Discipline Consensus Report
    https://all4ed.org/wp-content/uploads/2014/12/Nina_Salomon_School_Discipline_Consensus_Report.pdf
- Fix School Discipline Toolkit for Educators
    http://www.fixschooldiscipline.org/educator-toolkit

CHAPTER 17

Companion Article: The Value of Asian American Pre-K–12 Urban Education Principals

A Human Resources Developmental Perspective on the Barriers and Opportunity Pathways for America's "Model Minority"

Nicholas D. Hartlep

GOAL

The purpose of this companion guide exercise is to use Hughes's (2009) "people as technology" human resources development conceptual model in a practical way as it applies to hiring Asian American principals.

BACKGROUND

There is a desperate need for urban school districts to hire Asian American principals. Asian American students are the fastest-growing populations (López, Ruiz, & Patten, 2017), requiring an increased number of Asian American teachers and school administrators.

THEORY TO PRACTICE

The data inform us that Asian American principals are in need. Hughes's (2009) "people as technology" human resources development conceptual model can be seen in figure 17.1. The components of the model, seen in figure 17.2, are what you will be drawing from for this activity.

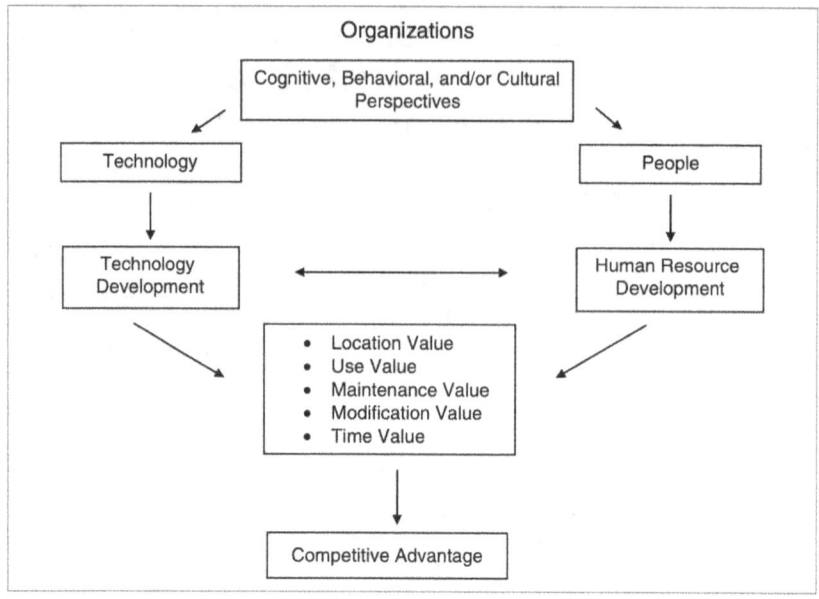

Figure 17.1. People as Technology Conceptual Model. Source: Hughes (2009)

Values	Technology Development	Human Resource Development
Location	Capital expense Engineering expertise Infrastructure changes	Cohesiveness in assigned environment Organizational culture Career development
Use	Often, it is known, upfront, how a piece of equipment is to be used before purchasing. Process control Strategic planning	Selection strategy Person–job fit Job analysis
Maintenance	Preventive maintenance systems and processes Investment in new tools	Training and development Motivation
Modification	Upgrades Slight modification Investment to ensure value is derived from this piece of equipment.	Growth and change Job enrichment Organization development
Time	Lifespan of equipment Depreciation of equipment expense	Length of time in position Downsizing or rightsizing

Figure 17.2. Components of People as Technology Conceptual Model. Source: Hughes (2009)

ACTIVITIES

1. Search for a principal job posting online. Try and locate one in an urban school district. Once you find one, print it and put it to the side. We will come back to it.
2. Conduct research on why Asian Americans are underrepresented in P–12 leadership positions. Create an annotated bibliography of scholarship on Asian American P–12 leadership. What themes emerge?
3. Interview an urban school district human resource officer, a principal, and a teacher. Your goal is to ask them how many Asian American P–12 leaders there are in their school, their district, and their state. Ask them ways these numbers could be increased.
4. Interview an Asian American principal. Ask them questions about their experience and their pathway to becoming a principal. Were there stumbling blocks? Were there stepping-stones?
5. Return to the job posting you printed. Where did you locate the job posting? Do you think it was a space that would lead an Asian American candidate to find it? If not, why not? Using the components in figure 17.2, rewrite the job post in a way that would be more friendly to an Asian American principal candidate. Find alternative places where you could post a job position for a principal position that would yield more Asian American applicants.
6. Print a copy of the materials you came up with in item 4 as well as any of the materials found in the "Additional Resources" section of this companion guide and share it with a colleague. If you have a colleague who makes hiring decisions, especially try to meet with him or her. Get coffee with this colleague and process the materials with him or her. Armed with this new knowledge, what can be done to increase the number of Asian American teachers and principals?

REFLECTION

What responsibility do you have for studying and understanding why there are so few Asian American principals in the United States? Asian Americans are routinely stereotyped as "model minorities" (Hartlep,

2013). How many friends of yours are Asian Americans? If you are a teacher, how many of your fellow teachers are Asian Americans? Howard (2016) writes that "we can't teach what we don't know." If you do not know a lot about Asian Americans and the issues impacting their personal and professional lives, what responsibility do you have for reading and reaching out to them? What is one thing you can commit to doing that can increase your knowledge, awareness, and empathy for Asian American P–12 leaders and their unique struggles within urban education?

REFERENCES

Hartlep, N. D. (2013). *The model minority stereotype: Demystifying Asian American success*. Charlotte, NC: Information Age.

Howard, G. R. (2016). *We can't teach what we don't know: White teachers, multiracial schools*. New York: Teachers College Press.

Hughes, C. (2009). "People as technology" conceptual model: Toward a new value creation paradigm for strategic human resource development. *Human Resource Development Review*, *9*(1), 48–71. http://citeseerx.ist.psu.edu/viewdoc/download?doi=10.1.1.857.9814&rep=rep1&ty pe=pdf.

López, G., Ruiz, N. G., & Patten, E. (2017, September 8). Key facts about Asian Americans, a diverse and growing population. Pew Research Center. https://www.pewresearch.org/fact-tank/2017/09/08/key-facts-about-asian-americans.

ADDITIONAL RESOURCES

Readers may find the following resources valuable:

- Leadership Academy and Urban Network Chicago (LAUNCH)
    The Leadership Academy and Urban Network for Chicago's aspiring principals (LAUNCH) was an early principal preparation program, designed to support and develop aspiring principals for Chicago Public Schools (CPS). LAUNCH targeted strong assistant principals within CPS schools in addition to identifying teacher leaders and other high-potential individuals who met the basic requirements of a master's degree, an administrative certificate, and at least six years of teaching experience. As candidates were al-

ready certified, the program targeted the development of key competencies through a five-week intensive program at the Kellogg Graduate School of Management at Northwestern University and a semester-long full-time apprenticeship with a mentor principal. https://thefundchicago.org/portfolio/leadership-academy-urban-network- chicago-launch.

- Professional Standards for Educational Leaders

    The Professional Standards for Educational Leaders provide guideposts that will help school leaders make a difference every day in the learning and well-being of students. Grounded in current research and the real-life experiences of educational leaders, they articulate the leadership that our schools need and that our students deserve. They are student-centric, outlining foundational principles of leadership to guide the practice of educational leaders so they can move the needle on student learning and achieve more equitable outcomes. They're designed to ensure that educational leaders are ready to meet the challenges of the job today and in the future as education, schools, and society continue to transform.

- Asian American & Pacific Islander Alliances (Teach for America)

    The effort to end educational inequity must include the leadership of individuals who share similar backgrounds with the students most affected by the injustice, and it should be led by those with personal proximity to the problem and its complexity. That's why we launched the Asian American and Pacific Islander (AAPI) Alliances in 2014. It's crucial that we grow our base of Asian American, Native Hawaiian, and Pacific Islander (AANHPI) teachers in order to better reflect our nation's AANHPI students and anticipate the changing student demographics in our schools. Teach For America's AAPI Alliances works alongside other organizations committed to deliver on the promise of equal opportunity for every child and help grow the leadership of AANHPI educators inside and outside of the classroom. We aim to mobilize a connected, thriving, culturally competent and community-responsive AANHPI leadership coalition working to advance educational equity for all children. https://www.teachforamerica.org/life-in-the-corps/your-tfa-network/asian-american-pacific-islander-alliances.

- Districts Matter: Cultivating the Principals Urban Schools Need (2013)

  This is a 2013 report published by the Wallace Foundation. According to the report, the school district profoundly shapes the destinies of its principals: how they are trained, hired, mentored, evaluated, and developed on the job. Yet until recently, many educators and policymakers overlooked the unique role districts can play to help principals shoulder their central responsibility: improving teaching and learning. Armed with new evidence about the importance of school leadership and how it can best be developed, a growing number of large districts are seeking to cultivate first-rate principals for all their schools. Doing so requires that they carry out two big tasks. First, build a large corps of well-qualified candidates for the principalship:

  Create job descriptions that clearly spell out what principals need to know and do to drive better instruction.
  Improve "preservice" principal training.
  Establish selective hiring procedures that identify the most promising future leaders and match them to the right schools.
  Ensure that hard-to-staff schools get top-quality leaders.

  Second, support school leaders on the job:

  Develop fair, reliable performance evaluations that hold principals accountable for student progress and inform their ongoing training.
  Offer mentoring to novice principals and professional development to all principals so that school leaders improve throughout their careers.
  Provide school leaders with timely, useful data and training on how to use those data.
  Enable principals to devote sufficient time to improving instruction and to making the best use of that time.
  Plan for orderly turnover and leadership succession

https://www.wallacefoundation.org/knowledge-center/Documents/Districts-Matter-Cultivating-the-Principals-Urban-Schools-Need.pdf.
- The Asian Educators Alliance (AsEA)

The Asian Educators Alliance (AsEA) is an Asian affinity organization committed to creating opportunities for Asian Pacific Islander South Asian(APISA) teachers and school staff to meet, network, identify challenges they face as APISA educators, discuss strategies to address these challenges, build mentoring structures, and share ways to support APISA families at our schools. AsEA was formed by APISA educators at San Francisco Bay Area independent schools in December 2004. In September 2006, a group of Asian educators in the New York Metropolitan Area created AsEANY, a New York affiliate of the organization. The AsEA annual conference is the only national conference that provides a space for APISA educators in independent, charter, and public schools to professionally network, mentor one another, develop leadership within their community, and strategize around challenges faced by APISA educators and families in their school. http://asianeducatorsalliance.weebly.com/about-us.html.

CHAPTER 18

Companion Article: Understanding the Politics of Race, Equity, and Neoliberalism in Everyday Leadership

Sarah Diem, Anjalé D. Welton,
Sarah W. Walters, and Shannon Paige Clark

GOAL

In a time of rising inequality, U.S. public schools are in dire need of antiracist educational leaders who are trained and prepared to critically unpack how the racial politics in their district and school community can affect their decision making and leadership practice. School leaders must be intentional in confronting how policies and practices are color evasive and market driven if they desire an education system that is antiracist and just for all students. The goal of the activities provided in our companion guide is to assist school leaders in being well positioned to actualize antiracist school agendas in neoliberal education contexts.

BACKGROUND

Color-evasive rhetoric and politics *and* neoliberal forces in education have denigrated the meaning of equity, particularly in urban school districts where leaders often use the language of equity and diversity but continue to acquiesce to the demands of those with more power (i.e., affluent, White individuals). Neoliberal policies and initiatives present across much of urban education ultimately negate any visions that urban districts may have to achieve racial equity. The market-driven policies and practices currently implemented in education are color evasive, as they use capitalist strategies that pretend to be race neutral but that, in reality, have significant racial implications that preserve the racial status quo. These policies and practices fail to take into consideration the different needs in various school contexts and serve only to perpetuate extant racial inequities (see Milner, 2010, 2012). And while we desperately need antiracist educational leaders in public schools, a leader is not antiracist in practice if they play some role in advancing neoliberal policies that in no way support but rather obstruct the educational opportunities and pathways of students of color. We believe that school leaders need to fully commit to implementing policies and practices that support students of color and create a more just education system for all students.

THEORY TO PRACTICE

We offer for consideration an antiracist policy decision-making protocol for educational leaders (see Diem & Welton, 2021) that we believe can assist in revealing the systemic racism existent in public schools that is a result of color-evasive, market-driven educational policies. Below we outline the six steps of the protocol that school leaders can work through as they examine the racial implications of policies and practices in their school communities:

1. *Assemble the appropriate team.* Include leaders from various sectors who can commit to collaborating toward an antiracist system, paying attention to include members with diverse backgrounds as well as leaders representative of the student population/community.
2. *Set expectations for the team.* Set goals, rules, and norms before the team's work commences.
3. *Understand the sociopolitical and racial context of the district and community.* Look for race-related patterns in order to understand how racism influences leadership and policy in your district and community.
4. *Conduct a critical policy review.* Center the perspectives of racially minoritized people, interrogate the distribution of resources and power, and hold people with power accountable for policy outcomes (Horsford, Scott, & Anderson, 2019).

5. *Conduct a critical leadership review.* Consider how democratic decision-making efforts are taking place within the school and community.
6. Summarize, (re)assess, and take action.

ACTIVITIES

1. In a fishbowl discussion, ask families, students, and community members to describe problematic practices and policies while school and district leaders listen. School and district leaders should then reflect on what they heard without justifying extant practices or policies *and* affirm the perspectives of families, students, and community members.
2. Utilizing a design thinking process, convene a racially diverse group of school stakeholders to generate ideas for an antiracist school with antiracist practices and policies.

REFLECTION

Critically reflect on and critique policies significant to your school community. Use the following questions to facilitate the discussion with your leadership team, faculty, and staff:

1. What are the roots and assumptions of our policies?
2. Which resources are distributed (un)equally or (in)equitably? What does this look like?
3. Is [insert name of policy] color evasive? How so?
4. Is [insert name of policy] market driven? How does this impact equity outcomes?
5. Is [insert name of policy] racially just? Why or why not? How do we know?
6. Is [insert name of policy] ethical? Why or why not? How do we know?
7. Is [insert name of policy] antiracist? Why or why not? How do we know?

REFERENCES

Diem, S., & Welton, A.D. (2021). *Anti-racist educational leadership and policy: Addressing racism in public education.* New York: Routledge.

Horsford, S. D., Scott, J. T., & Anderson, G. L. (2019). *The politics of education policy in an era of inequality: Possibilities for democratic schooling.* New York: Routledge.

Milner, H. R., IV. (2010). What does teacher education have to do with teaching? Implications for diversity studies. *Journal of Teacher Education, 61*(1–2), 118–131.

Milner, H. R., IV. (2012). Beyond a test score: Explaining opportunity gaps in educational practice. *Journal of Black Studies, 43*(6), 693–718.

ADDITIONAL RESOURCES

- Great Lakes Equity Assistance Center Policy Equity Analysis Toolkit
    https://greatlakesequity.org/sites/default/files/201625031354_equity_tool.pdf
- National Coalition on School Diversity Issue Brief 6, *Prioritizing School Integration in ESSA State Implementation Plans*
    https://school-diversity.org/pdf/DiversityIssueBriefNo6.pdf
- Portland Public Schools Racial Equity and Social Justice Lens
    https://www.pps.net/Page/2305
- Rallis, S., Rossman, G., Reagan, T., Cobb, C., & Kuntz, A. (2008). *Leading dynamic schools: How to create and implement ethical policies.* Thousand Oaks, CA: Corwin Press.

Part VI

TRANSNATIONALISM

CHAPTER 19

Companion Article: Supporting Undocumented Students

Principals Taking Action

Sofia Bahena, Brianda De Leon, and Mariela A. Rodríguez

GOAL

The purpose of the exercises and information in this companion guide chapter are to inform those in the educational community and beyond of the importance for the need to understand the rights of students who are undocumented. Here, via the background and course activities, we discuss specific action items school leaders and students can take to best support students who are undocumented.

BACKGROUND

It is important for school leaders, teachers, counselors, and educational support staff to be fully informed of the rights of students who are undocumented. In this way, the school can be a "safe" space for students to focus on their academic growth without fear. All students attending public schools in the United States are entitled to a free and appropriate public education. Thus, educators at the school level have the task of providing academic programs that promote high-quality instruction for all students, including students who are undocumented. Providing academic instruction to such students isn't only a mandate but also an ethical and moral obligation. The field of education encompasses not only instructional goals but also the emotional well-being of students. Therefore, we encourage principals to use the following recommendations to enhance program offerings and support services for students who are undocumented in their schools.

TEACHING AND LEARNING EXPERIENCES

- School leaders must be aware of immigration policies and support the rights of students who are undocumented and their families.
- Teachers can purposefully engage students who are undocumented in the curriculum. Students need to "see" themselves in the books they read and in the assignments they complete. In this way, students' experiences are validated.
- Students must take active roles in classroom discussions and activities. Teachers need to create such opportunities and spaces.
- School librarians can make purposeful book purchases to increase the availability of books that portray the lived experiences of students who are undocumented and of books in languages other than English.
- Communication between the school staff and families must be made available in languages other than English. If e-mails or other electronic formats are used, then school leaders must make concerted efforts to make free Wi-Fi and/or school computer labs available for parents to be able to read the e-mails.
- All school staff must be aware of community resources to support undocumented students and their families so that everyone has the knowledge to connect families with the resources that they need.

DISCUSSION QUESTIONS

1. How can school leaders create the conditions necessary in a school for students who are undocumented and their families to thrive?
2. What are ways in which teachers can create "safe spaces" in their classrooms for students who are undocumented to feel valued and to thrive academically?
3. In which ways do teachers, counselors, and school leaders communicate with the families of students who are undocumented?
4. What programs does your school district have in place to support students who are undocumented and the families of those students? Are these programs effective? What evidence do you have to support this?

5. What types of professional development and training does your school district offer teachers, counselors, and school leaders related to effective practices that support students who are undocumented? How many of these training sessions have you participated in? To what extent did you apply what you learned?
6. If your school district does not have programs in place to support students who are undocumented and the families of those students, then what actions can you take to change that?

Using an Equity Tool

There are some aspects of the teaching and learning process that school leaders can address that are directly related to supporting students who are undocumented:

- Create a team of advocates for students who are undocumented that includes students, school leaders, counselors, teachers, support staff, and community stakeholders.
- The team will help to develop the school's mission statement that clearly articulates specific goals for students who are undocumented.
- The team can guide other members of the school community in enacting key practices that support students who are undocumented both academically and emotionally.
- Team members can conduct a "walk-through" of the campus to see what the physical spaces looks like. These include the path leading to the main doors of the campus, hallways, classrooms, library, and recreation areas. Is the campus a welcoming space? If so, for whom?
- Create opportunities for students who are undocumented to share their successes and challenges. These could include student advocacy clubs, small-group platicás coordinated by school counselors, and after-school activities with families held in the *comunidad*.

ADDITIONAL RESOURCES

- American Civil Liberties Union
  https://www.aclu.org
- Civil Rights Project/Proyecto Derechos Civiles
  https://civilrightsproject.ucla.edu/about-us
- Immigrant Legal Resource Center
  https://www.ilrc.org
- Mexican American Legal Defense and Educational Fund
  https://www.maldef.org
- Crawford, E. R. (2017). The ethic of community and incorporating undocumented immigrant concerns into ethical school leadership. *Educational Administration Quarterly, 53*(2), 147–179.
- Crawford, E. R., & Fishman-Weaver, K. (2016). Proximity and policy: Negotiating safe spaces between immigration policy and school practice. *International Journal of Qualitative Studies in Education, 29*(3), 273–296.
- Crawford, E. R., & Valle, F. (2016). Educational justice for undocumented students: How school counselors encourage student persistence in schools. *Education Policy Analysis Archives, 24*(98), 1–25.
- Crawford, E. R., & Witherspoon Arnold, N. (2017). "We don't talk about undocumented status. . . . We talk about helping children": How school leaders shape school climate for undocumented immigrants. *IJELM, 5*(2), 116–147.
- Jaffe-Walter, R., Patton Miranda, C., & Lee, S. J. (2019). From protest to protection: Navigating politics with immigrant students in uncertain times. *Harvard Educational Review, 89*(2), 251–276.
- Koyama, J., & Kasper, J. (2020). Pushing the boundaries: Education leaders, mentors, and refugee students. *Educational Administration Quarterly.* https://doi.org/10.1177/0013161X20914703.
- Valdivia, C., & Clark-Ibañez, M. (2018). "It is hard right now": High school educators working with undocumented students. *Latino Public Policy, 10.* https://scholar.smu.edu/latino-policy/10.

CHAPTER 20

Companion Article: Conceptualizing Equity in a Borderland Language Ecology

Magdalena Pando

GOAL

The purpose of this exercise is to apply a borderland language ecology into an educational context to promote linguistic equity for borderland emerging bilinguals learning science. Borderland entities in a language ecology share common properties and languaging processes, such as translanguaging. A borderland language ecology models ways of translanguaging in communication that can be leveraged in the classroom to promote linguistic equity in urban areas with high percentages of (but not limited to) English learners (ELs).

BACKGROUND

Assessment data for the United States in the past 10 years (Office of English Language Acquisition, 2019) have revealed persistent performance gaps in science scores for ELs in grades 4, 8, and 12 when compared to non-ELs. Standards-based reform (National Governors Association Center for Best Practices, 2010; NGSS Lead States, 2013) aim to promote equal access to a quality education for all students. Since the inception of reform efforts identified here, performance gaps have not indicated significant change in favor of the EL group. This companion guide proposes a theory-to-practice application of a borderland language ecology to science education with ELs. This chapter and companion guide problematize the term *English learner*. It is problematic in that English is the sole language attributed power through use of the term. Unrecognized, though, is the fact that ELs are bilingual if not multilingual (and multimodal) learners. As a result, hereinafter, the term *emerging bilingual (EB)* is used.

THEORY TO PRACTICE

Common to many educators and administrators is the use of English-language learning activities and strategies, such as the use of anchor charts, word walls, visual scaffolding, vocabulary flip books, and graphic organizers, to name a few. While well intended, English-language development strategies privilege the English language and hence foster monoglossic perspectives to language use. This power attributed to the English language often excludes the culturally and linguistically diverse epistemologies (ways of knowing and constructing knowledge) of the EB student in the classroom. Standards-based reforms promote science literacy for all (NGSS Lead States, 2013) through scientific and engineering practices that include constructing science explanations, evidence-based arguments, and models to represent phenomena. These are content-specific and language-intensive tasks that are not well scaffolded through traditional English-language learning strategies. A borderland language ecology considers all entities and their common translanguaging practices when mediating experience (in this guide, science learning). Next are some activities for including EBs' culturally and linguistically diverse contributions in science learning.

ACTIVITIES

1. Translanguaging is common in a borderland language ecology and can be used as a pedagogical tool in science to allow EBs to use their linguistic repertoire for mediating science learning experiences during inquiry investigations. Identify some non-traditional language teaching strategies that foster collaborative spaces for translanguaging in interactive activities among EBs. Think of some ways to scaffold content-specific languaging tasks through translanguaging as a pedagogical tool.

2. Scientific modeling is the process of constructing models to represent scientific phenomena, testing them (by gathering data as evidence), and evaluating them. To evaluate models is to engage in a critique of what they represent. This requires EBs to design a model and explain it to their peers to persuade them that their model is an adequate correspondence of the science phenomenon being represented. Identify strategies you could use to foster translanguaging spaces of collaboration to engage EBs in multimodal representations of knowledge through the modeling process in a science lesson.
3. *Teacher project.* You are planning a lesson on heat transfer. You set up a lab demonstration where you place an ice cube under a heat lamp and allow students to observe.
    a. What model do you anticipate your EBs constructing or drawing? What materials will you provide them to construct (or draw) their models?
    b. EBs will be expected to explain their model design to each other to persuade their peers that their individual model design is an adequate correspondence of the effect of heat on the ice cube. Their explanation of their model depends on this persuasive task. What scaffolds will you use to support their explanation task?
    c. As you plan steps a and b in your project, reflect on how you are enacting linguistic equity for your EBs through translanguaging spaces of collaboration. How does your selection of translanguaging activities and strategies include your EBs' contributions to knowledge in science learning?
4. *Administrator project.* Read steps 1 through 3 for a teacher at your campus who you are evaluating. You have prior knowledge that the language of instruction is English on the day you observe the teacher. You notice the teacher using native language support activities, and you listen to several EBs alternating between English and Spanish as they point to and write in their models and talk to each other. You see most students actively engaged in the lesson. How will you enact linguistic equity to support your teacher as you provide him or her with areas of refinement and reinforcement as a result of your observation and evaluation?

REFLECTION

The meaning of leadership in this guide is extended to what it means to lead through languaging. Languaging requires use of some form of language (gestural/verbal) as a cultural artifact to mediate experience. While mediating experience, students, teachers, administrators, and policymakers are encouraged to rethink how they lead in their roles. Students require opportunities to language, and for the borderland EB, translanguaging is a common way of mediating his or her experience. Why not let them lead their own mediation of experience by affording them their linguistic right to communicate through translanguaging? This languaging style should be validated as a linguistic asset by teachers, administrators, and policymakers. Educational stakeholders are leaders who shape (or rather control) the language of instruction through policy. Language of instruction allocation in language instruction educational programs resists the way in which EBs may translanguage through the use of more than one language. English is not undermined here, as it is equally important for EBs to develop their English-language proficiency. However, EBs should not experience feelings of inferiority to the privileging of English only during language of instruction in English. This companion guide calls on the teacher, the administrator, and the policymaker to reflect on their leadership through linguistic equity. How will your leadership influence linguistic equity or inequity? To language or not to language? This is the essential question we should ask ourselves as we lead to enact our roles as educational stakeholders.

REFERENCES

National Governors Association Center for Best Practices, Council of Chief State School Officers. (2010). *Common Core State Standards*. http://www.corestandards.org.

NGSS Lead States. (2013). *Next Generation Science Standards: For states, by states*. Washington, DC: National Academies Press.

Office of English Language Acquisition. (2019). *Fast fact: English learners and science achievement*. https://ncela.ed.gov/files/fast_facts/FactSheet_Del4.4_Science_120419_508.pdf.

ADDITIONAL RESOURCES

- Clement, J. J., & Rea-Ramirez, M. A. (2008). *Model based learning and instruction in science: Models and modeling in science education.* New York: Springer.
- Duschl, R. A., & Bismack, A. S. (2016). *Reconceptualizing STEM education: The central role of practices.* New York: Routledge.
- García, O., & Kleifgen, A. (2018). *Educating emergent bilinguals: Policies, programs, and practices for English learners.* New York: Teachers College Press.
- Osborne, J. (2010). Arguing to learn in science: The role of collaborative, critical discourse. *Science, 328*(5977), 463–466.

CHAPTER 21

Companion Article: Projecting the Voices of the Voiceless

Undocumented Students in a Southwest Borderland K–12 School District

Roberto Lozano

GOAL

The goal of this activity is for educational leaders to reflect on and devise a plan of action on how they can create spaces in their learning communities where students have the opportunity to develop strong, trusting relationships with all stakeholders at their schools. My hope is that by doing this, students who have historically been marginalized view their schools as safe learning environments where they feel welcomed and have the opportunity to achieve their full academic potential.

BACKGROUND

The stories of Alejandro, Carmen, and Raul revealed the importance of relationships and mentorship as a factor that contributed to the successful attainment of their high school diplomas. Their lived experiences revealed that once they developed strong, trusting relationships with one of their teachers, they had the courage to disclose their immigration status. In a study that examined the effects of student trust in teacher and student perceptions of safety identification with school, Mitchell, Kensler, and Tschannen-Moran (2016) emphasized the important role of the school leader in setting the tone of the school and establishing a climate of trust. For leaders to set a climate of trust, they must be self-reflective and have the ability to self-monitor how their leadership is influencing a culture of trust. To accomplish this, I recommend that leaders utilize a self-reflective journal. Much like a researcher, school leaders would benefit from using a self-reflective journal to track their efforts and reflect on what has worked and what has not. More important, their self-reflective data can help leaders develop a plan of action to ensure that trust is built within their schools' communities.

THEORY TO PRACTICE

Using a self-reflective journal is a strategy that can facilitate reflexivity, whereby researchers use their journal to examine "personal assumptions and goals" and clarify "individual belief systems and subjectivities" (Ortlipp, 2008). Much like researchers, I posit that by creating a self-reflective journal, school leaders will engage in and practice reflexivity where their personal assumptions and goals are documented.

ACTIVITIES

The actions outlined below will assist educational leaders in effectively using a self-reflective journal.

Time to Write and Reflect

Set aside at least two or three times a week to write in your self-reflective journal. If possible, this time should be uninterrupted and should be part of your weekly routine. It may be hard for this to become a routine, so a suggestion would be to allot time in small increments: start with five minutes and then gradually extend the time. The more time you spend on reflecting and writing, the richer data you will have.

Guiding Questions

When writing in your self-reflective journal, address the following guiding questions to assist you in reflecting:

1. What actions did I take this week that contributed to creating a climate of trust within the school community?

2. What are three positive indicators that I observed this week from my staff or students that are evidence that the school is moving toward a climate of trust?
3. What is one action and/or area that I observed that did not contribute to moving the school toward a climate of trust?
4. What action will I take next week to address the action and/or area that did not contribute to moving the school toward a climate of trust?

Data to Action

Your reflective journal entries should be used as a powerful data source that can assist you in developing a concrete plan of action for your school community. Use the data collected to find what procedures, actions, programs, or initiatives have contributed to developing a school climate of trust. It is also important to share your findings with someone else within your school community who has a leadership role. This could be a teacher leader, an assistant principal, or a group of students who are in leadership roles. Conversing about the data you gathered with others can also assist you in refining the steps you will take to ensure that a climate of trust is established within your school community.

REFLECTION

As evidenced by the interviews of the participants in this chapter, it is critical that school leaders find innovative ways to ensure that they create trusting and safe school communities. Using a self-reflective journal is a strategy that will contribute to a school leader's efforts to create a school climate of trust where all students, regardless of their backgrounds, will be afforded the opportunity to achieve their full academic potential.

REFERENCES

Mitchell, R. M., Kensler, L., & Tschannen-Moran, M. (2016). Student trust in teachers and student perceptions of safety: Positive predictors of student identification with school. *International Journal of Leadership in Education.* doi:10.1080/13603124.2016.1157211.

Ortlipp, M. (2008). Keeping and using reflective journals in the qualitative research process. *Qualitative Report, 13*(4), 695–705.

CHAPTER 22

Companion Article: "They Don't Even Know Me"

Effects of the Model Minority Myth on Asian American Students in a Southwest Borderland High School

Jennifer Maya Haan

GOAL

As educational leaders, we have a responsibility to engage in a process of inquiry that results in a deeper understanding of the student population that we serve (Santamaría & Santamaría, 2011). It was evident from the Asian American student participants that this was the first time an adult at the school was interested in their experiences. The stories told by Anayeli, Jessica, and Lily revealed that our youth must not be silenced. Asian American students' stories must be told, and we must hear them. An ideal way to hear voices is to conduct student focus groups on your own campus.

BACKGROUND

Jones and Yonezawa (2005) posited that listening to diverse students discuss their learning helps educators confront their own assumptions about students' capabilities and motivations. These assumptions are often a result of unintentional negative preconceptions about students' race, ethnicity, and culture; therefore, it is imperative that educators practice "radical listening" (Guo & Vulchi, 2019). This practice challenges us to "ask for people's soul stories about their identity . . . tune out our internal dialogues . . . and actually listen" (p. 195). Conducting focus groups with students is perceived to be time consuming given the many tasks of a high school administrator. I argue that conducting a focus group may save educational leaders' time in achieving three goals: (1) strengthen relationships with students, (2) identify potential issues facing any other students of color, and (3) gather data to present to district leaders to advocate for additional resources for your school-based programs.

THEORY TO PRACTICE

Kinzie (2016) explained that focus groups provide an ideal way to engage student participants. Focus groups can lead to rich conversation and meaningful insights into issues. Moreover, focus groups can assist in understanding a variety of perspectives as well as provide support and credence for emerging themes (Kinzie, 2016; Merriam & Tisdell, 2016). The value of focus groups rests in the interaction that takes place among participants. These truths more readily emerged in a synergistic format by allowing students to share their experiences in a confidential setting.

ACTIVITIES

The following actions can help you conduct student focus groups on your campus.

Identification and Recruitment

Initially, no students volunteered or reached out to me as a result of classroom presentations, so I took another approach. I was assisted by a student as a liaison and spokesperson. I predicted that these students might trust a peer over an authority figure, especially because Jessica was going to be one of the participants who would take part in the focus group.

Focus Group Facilitation

When facilitating the focus group discussion, Kinzie (2016) recommended arranging seating so that participants can interact easily with one another and with the facilitator. The participants and I were seated around a table so that the session could become a conversation. Snacks and water were allowed in the focus group sessions because the sessions were held after school hours and the students had not eaten since lunch.

Building Rapport

Each participant was engaged in dialogue prior to the focus group session in order to establish rapport and place the participants at ease. I was explicit in stating that their responses would remain anonymous and that pseudonyms would be used in my report of findings. I allowed them to select the pseudonym of their choice. They giggled and smiled as they spent time playing "make-believe."

REFLECTION

The questions listed below may help you uncover and understand your reluctance in conducting student focus groups:

1. What could be a negative outcome in conducting a focus groups with students? What could be positive outcome?
2. What would be the reaction of faculty members and administrators if you were to suggest a focus group? What would be the reaction of parents and families?
3. Do you believe your role as an administrator would impede or enhance the ability to successfully facilitate a focus group with students? Why or why not?

REFERENCES

Guo, W., & Vulchi, P. (2019). *Tell me who you are: Sharing our stories of race, culture, and identity.* New York: TarcherPerigee.

Jones, M., & Yonezawa, S. (2005). Inviting students to analyze their learning experience. In M. Pollack (Ed.), *Everyday anti-racism: Getting real about race in schools* (pp. 212–216). New York: New Press.

Kinzie, J. (2016). Focus groups. In F. K. Stage & K. Manning (Eds.), *Research in the college context: Approaches and methods* (pp. 62–78). New York: Routledge.

Merriam, S. B., & Tisdell, E. J. (2016). *Qualitative research: A guide to design and implementation.* San Francisco, CA: Jossey-Bass.

Santamaria, L., & Santamaria, A. P. (2011). *Applied critical leadership in education: Choosing change.* London: Routledge.

CHAPTER 23

Companion Article: A Metaphor Analysis of Tragedy and Trauma

Educational Leadership Responses to Addressing Transnationalistic Terror and Racial Violence

Azadeh F. Osanloo, Sarah Jane Baker, Kristine Andrea Velásquez, Rick Marlatt, and Noelle Witherspoon Arnold

GOAL

The goal of these activities is to analyze how urban educational leaders utilize their language in addressing acts of violence impacting their educational communities. Creating conscious awareness of word choices when referencing traumatic events can ultimately aid in creating a supportive and inclusive educational setting. In addition, this companion guide is geared toward preparing the educational leader's mind-set for being empathetic to the experiences of their students, colleagues, and educational community.

BACKGROUND

Educational leaders must confront the challenges associated with responding to racism, racial violence, gun violence, and terror that impacts their educational community. Unfortunately, students and teachers must live through trauma on a daily basis, and it is important that their schools help them comprehend their experiences (Engebretson & Weiss, 2015). Some major recent events that impacted school communities included the mass shooting at Walmart in El Paso, Texas, in 2019, which was geared toward murdering as many Hispanics as possible. Another is the police brutality and murder of an innocent Black man named George Floyd in 2020. School leaders must be equipped with expressing their support of their communities and must do so in an empathetic manner in order to create meaningful change (Boske, Osanloo, & Newcomb, 2017).

THEORY TO PRACTICE

The activities below will draw on empathetic leadership in order to assist educational leaders with comprehending what is needed in their language to showcase support of their educational community. Through this activity, educational leaders will become mindful of their words and communication toward each unique population and groups of individuals. They will be conscious of the manner in which they discuss traumatic events to show respect to the sensitive matters of vulnerable groups.

The activities allow for the explicit evaluation and reflection of language in the communication that educational leaders utilize with their school communities. It will ultimately equip educational leaders with the ability to think consciously of the experiences that people face, especially if their experiences are different than their own.

ACTIVITIES

1. *Role playing.* You are a principal of a popular high school in a highly diverse urban city. You are very well known, and the community continually looks up to you for guidance because of your empathetic leadership reputation. Unfortunately, a series of hate crimes has been impacting your community, and your students and parents do not feel safe returning to school. Sixty percent of your student population is considered economically disadvantaged, 60 percent are women, 10 percent are considered as having limited English proficiency, and 90 percent are considered minorities.

    The local news has reached out to you for an interview to see how you will handle the situation. Students and parents want to know what you will say and about action steps that will be taken to keep them safe. Prepare a five-minute speech on live television:

- Identify what you will say to your students, their parents, and the community.
- Create a strategic plan to keep your school safe and reveal this plan during your speech.
- Ensure that your leadership is empathetic in this devastating time.
- Record your speech and review it.
- Share your recorded speech with a trusted colleague or friend and seek feedback on what you could have done differently to improve.

2. *Reflection.* Identify tragic events that have impacted your institution. This can include the murder of George Floyd, the hate crime that occurred at the El Paso Walmart, or any other tragic event that has occurred close to your community and school. Reflect on communication that was released by the leaders of your institution on these tragedies. Answer the following questions:
    - Was there communication between the institution and the educational community on the tragedies?
        - If not, why? Who should have provided a statement? Why didn't they? What can be done to ensure that your educational community feels safe and included despite the lack of communication? How can you change the lack of communication?
    - What media were utilized in this communication (e.g., social media posts, e-mails, news statements, newspaper articles, etc.)?
    - Who delivered the communication?
        - Was it a group of individuals or individual leaders?
    - Was the communication empathetic?
        - How or how not?
    - Were victims named and honored?
        - Was naming the victims considered important?
    - Were the responses vague and "safe," or did they explicitly state important terms, such as *racism* and *hate crimes*?
    - What would you have recommended to the institution on this communication?

- What would you have changed in terms of language and communication?
- Who would you have expected to release a statement but did not?
- What action should accompany the released statements?
- How can the success of these proposed actions be measured?
3. *Know your institution.* It is important to understand who the students, faculty, and staff who encompass your institution are to be empathetic toward their needs and be ready to communicate appropriately at any given moment:
- Create a list of the demographics of your institution.
- Create a list of the demographics of the city in which your institution resides.
- Identify if your institution is a direct reflect of its city's population. Do the percentages match? If not, identify what the reasons are and determine how you can diversity your institution.
- Create a list of the different genders and ethnicities of students, faculty, and staff that encompass your institution.
  - Research and become acquainted with the struggles and barriers that each population and group face.
  - Look up typical macroaggressions and microaggressions faced within educational systems.
  - Identify if there is anything you can do different to improve your institution and their experiences.
- Write down five ways in which you commit to take action to improve the experiences of your institution's population. Show this list to your supervisor and determine how you can work together to accomplish your list.

REFLECTION

- Lack of research exists regarding the language of educational leaders in response to tragedy and trauma in higher-education institutions, particularly regarding Hispanic-serving institutions, which serve diverse populations. Take a moment to reflect on your own experience, if any, with tragedy and your position to

communicate necessary information to those who depend on you as a leader. How may you use those experiences for both research and practice?
- Unfortunately, tragic events are common in the world we live in. Consider the population of students you lead and reflect on their needs and required support systems when processing tragic events. Are you and/or your institution prepared to support each student? Are support practices as diverse as you may believe? Should you be more informed? How?
- In terms of conscious awareness in your own educational setting, reflect on how you may be better prepared to provide support and motivation to your students and community. Consider your definition of empathy; what are ways you, as an individual, may better impact students and community through your language during tragic and traumatic events?

REFERENCES

Boske, C., Osanloo, A., & Newcomb, W. S. (2017). Exploring empathy to promote social justice leadership in schools. *Journal of School Leadership*, *27*(3), 361–391. doi:10.1177/105268461702700303.

Engebretson, K. E., & Weiss, A. M. (2015). A brave new curriculum: Empowering teachers and students in times of trauma. *Curriculum and Teaching Dialogue*, *17*(1–2), 57–68.

About the Editors

René O. Guillaume, PhD, is an assistant professor and also serves as an interim codirector in the School of Teacher Preparation, Administration, and Leadership in the College of Education at New Mexico State University. He earned his undergraduate degree from the University of Texas at El Paso; his master's in education from Texas A&M University, with an emphasis in student affairs administration in higher education; and his PhD in educational leadership and administration from New Mexico State University. Prior to this appointment, he spent a decade working in numerous student services administration roles in postsecondary education, serving more recently as director for the TRIO Upward Bound program. His research interests include social justice issues in education, racial and ethnic identity development, and faculty teaching, life, and culture. He has more than 20 publications and has presented extensively.

Noelle Witherspoon Arnold, PhD, is associate dean for equity, diversity, and global engagement and professor of educational administration in the College of Education and Human Ecology at The Ohio State University. Prior to this appointment, she was director for the education doctorate program in educational administration in the Department of Educational Studies at Ohio State. She has written and presented extensively and has nine books published or in press and more than 70 publications. A former administrator at the district and state levels, she also serves as a consultant in the United States, advising districts on diversity and inclusion and teaching and leading in urban and rural contexts. Her research agenda terms context-based interdisciplinary research with a focus on disparities, which has yielded $2.3 million in internal and external funding. In addition, her scholarship was one of only four authors' works submitted to the U.S. Senate for Emerging Peer Reviewed Research on Educational Leadership, Policy, and Literacy in Black & Brown Communities. She was the first African American female to serve as president of the University Council for Educational Administration.

Azadeh F. Osanloo, PhD, is professor of educational leadership and administration and recently ended her term as the inaugural codirector of the School of Teacher Preparation, Administration, and Leadership in the College of Education at New Mexico State University. She was formerly the Stan Fulton Endowed Chair for the Improvement of Border and Rural Schools (2013–2018). She earned her undergraduate degree from the University of Wisconsin, Madison; her master's degree in public policy from the Wagner Graduate School of Public Service at New York University; and her PhD in educational leadership and policy studies from Arizona State University. Her research agenda focuses on issues of educational equity; educational leadership and policy; diversity, multiculturalism, and human rights; and social justice. She has published four coedited books and more than 40 reviewed publications and had more than 50 inter/national presentations. She has guided 30 doctoral students to the successful completion of their programs—all with studies that emphasize the core tenets of social justice leadership. In addition, she has worked to increase marginalized student representation in the STEM fields via school-community gardens and created the Youth Leadership Academy, a partnership with the Las Cruces Police Department designed to improve community and police relations. She has won the Dean's Awards for her teaching and service; is a 2015 recipient of the American Graduate Champion Award, an award bestowed by the Corporation for Public Broadcasting; and won the Ngage New Mexico Educator Award in 2017 for her social justice work at New Mexico State and in the community

About the Contributors

Douglas Allen is a PhD candidate at Florida State University studying affirmative resistance strategies to social injustice through placemaking. His interest in educational geographies began as a U.S. history teacher at an urban majority-minority high school and became the focus of his graduate work. Specifically, his work as a master's student in the history of race, ethnicity, and society and his doctoral research focused on black geographies have both engaged with affirmative place-making at historically black colleges and universities. His recent work looks at the production of Florida A&M University as a place of respite for Black students.

Elizabeth C. Apodaca is manager of the online instructional design team for the New Mexico State University Digital Learning Initiatives unit. Her team creates online courses and programs and facilitates professional development in online course planning, building, and delivery for faculty and staff. She is also a doctoral candidate in educational leadership and administration at New Mexico State. Her research interests focus on faculty of color, faculty service, and Latina representation in higher education. She lives with her two college-aged children, four dogs, and two cats. She is a native New Mexican who grew up in Santa Fe.

Sofia Bahena, EdD, is an assistant professor in the Department of Education Leadership and Policy Studies at the University of Texas at San Antonio. Her research interests include K–12 education policy, college access, program evaluation, and community–school relationships. She has experience working with English/Spanish bilingual communities, parents, and families and conducting both quantitative and qualitative analyses. She holds a BA in business administration and sociology from Trinity University (San Antonio) and an MEd in human development and psychology and EdD in cultures, communities, and education from the Harvard Graduate School of Education.

Sarah Jane Baker, PhD, is an educator and scholar. Her academic focus and motivation is derived from her doctoral studies centered on women in leadership positions and the metaphorical labyrinth of challenges that women in leadership overcome to reach their respective goals. Her work also examines the mean-girl phenomenon, academic mobbing, and gendered experiences in higher education. Prior to her work as a doctoral student, she served the College of Health and Social Services at New Mexico State University as a liaison advocating for student leadership, scholarship, and academic success. She earned her BA at Arizona State University and her MA and PhD at New Mexico State. Her student-centered motivation guides her to positively impact learners at all levels.

Randy Clinton Bell is a doctoral candidate in the bilingual/bicultural program of the College of Education at the University of Texas at Austin. A National Board–certified and former bilingual elementary school teacher, his research considers bilingualism in education broadly, with specific attention to how students' languaging practices intersect with global, racial, class, and gender subjectivities.

Risha Berry, PhD, is an assistant professor in the Department of Educational Leadership in the School of Education at Virginia Commonwealth University in Richmond, Virginia. She is affiliated faculty with the Institute for Inclusion, Inquiry, and Innovation's Urban Education and Family Core. She studies leadership in urban-serving community agencies and organizations. Her scholarship is focused on structural barriers to urban service leaders' career mobility and effectiveness. Her dynamic organizational leadership background includes a track record of developing successful public–private partnerships, designing organizational frameworks, and writing and securing numerous program grants totaling more than $1 million.

Bryant O. Best is a Russell G. Hamilton scholar, Peabody College fellow, and doctoral student in the Justice and Diversity in Education PhD program at Vanderbilt University. His research interests include urban education, culturally responsive teaching and leadership practices, and the school-to-prison pipeline. Prior to Vanderbilt, he served at the Council of Chief State School Officers and the American Council on Education, where he supported education leaders in K–12 and higher education, respectively, in finding solutions to some of the nation's most pressing questions of policy and practice.

Tobe C. Bott-Lyons, BA, New School for Social Research; MA, New Mexico Highlands University; and PhD, New Mexico State University, was born and raised in New Mexico. He is currently the director of the TRIO Upward Bound program at Northern New Mexico College. Prior to this, he worked in college student affairs, adult education, and community-based youth development. In 2020, he completed his PhD in educational leadership at New Mexico State University. His current research is focused primarily on policies, programs, and practices to promote and expand college access for underserved and marginalized students.

Joshua Childs is an assistant professor of education policy at the University of Texas at Austin. His research focuses on cross-sector collaborations to address complex educational issues. Specifically, his work examines how collaborative approaches have the potential to improve school attendance and academic achievement and reduce opportunity gaps for students in urban and rural schools.

Shelby Chipman, a native of Miami, Florida, is the director of bands and professor of music at Florida A&M University. Since his doctoral work at Florida State University, his research has focused on educator challenges of teaching in urban school districts. Before his appointment at Florida A&M, he taught music in the Miami-Dade County Public School system for 10 years. He has presented his research on supporting at-risk students in urban education at national conferences and is dedicated to urban education in research and practice.

Shannon Paige Clark is a doctoral candidate in the Department of Educational Policy Studies at the University of Illinois at Chicago. Shannon's experiences as an elementary educator and social worker inform her approach to research and fuel her commitment to reducing the research-practice gap. Shannon's research centers Black families and their interactions with teachers. She explores strategies and solutions that can benefit students, families, and communities that aren't served by the status quo.

Sheryl J. Croft, PhD, is an associate professor of educational leadership in the Bagwell College of Education of Kennesaw State University, director of the Doctorate Educational Leadership, and director of Teaching in the Urban South, a multistate affiliation of scholars dedicated to providing and ensuring educational opportunities for marginalized students throughout the Southeast. As a veteran practitioner with more than 35 years in education, she has served at every level of leadership, from principal to assistant school superintendent. As a scholar-practitioner, her work is informed by and lies at the intersectionality of informed practice and research that seeks to improve educational opportunities for students marginalized by systemic inequities.

Brianda De Leon is a third-year doctoral student at the University of Texas at San Antonio. She is originally from Long Beach, California, and is a proud daughter of immigrants from Zacatecas and Guerrero, Mexico. During her master's program at the University of Utah, she served as a graduate assistant at an Undocumented Student Resource Center, where she learned the complex relationship between education and immigration. Her research focuses on the establishment of Undocumented Student Resource Centers at public institutions of higher education.

Sarah Diem, PhD, is an associate professor in the Department of Educational Leadership and Policy Analysis at the University of Missouri. Her research focuses on the sociopolitical and geographic contexts of education, paying particular attention to how politics, leadership, and the implementation of educational policies affect outcomes related to equity, opportunity, and racial diversity within public schools.

Luis Esquivel is a student in the CACREP-accredited MA in Clinical Mental Health Counseling program at New Mexico State University. He earned his BS in psychology from Carroll University. His research interests include holistic approaches for clients experiencing comorbid chronic health and mental symptoms and discovering how practitioners can provide optimal care for clients by working on interdisciplinary teams to simultaneously meet their clients' mental and physical health care needs.

Christine Fagan, EdD, serves as special project manager in the Office of Equity, Diversity, and Global Engagement in the College of Education and Human Ecology at The Ohio State University.

Tomika Ferguson, PhD, is the interim assistant dean for student affairs and inclusive excellence and an assistant professor and co-coordinator of the EdD program in the Department of Educational Leadership at Virginia Commonwealth University's School of Education. Her scholarship examines the experiences of girls and women of color, intercollegiate athletics, issues of affordability and retention for low-income students and students of color, and the professional development of K–12 and nonprofit leaders around issues of equity and inclusion. Her work has been featured in *Diverse Issues in Higher Education*, the *Journal of College Student Development*, and the *College Student Affairs Journal*. She is the founder of the Black Athlete Sister Circle program, a holistic student development program for Black women student-athletes in higher education. She has professional experiences working in community partnerships, residence life, enrollment management, and nonprofit organizations. She received her bachelor's degree from the University of Virginia and her master's and doctoral degrees in higher education from Indiana University Bloomington.

Andrew C. Gray is a doctoral student in the Department of Sociology and Criminal Justice at the University of Delaware. His research interests include exploring how structural forces impact levels of crime and social control, including the role of race and racism. With his focus on race, he is also interested in examining racialized violence and social control and how these have persisted throughout history by taking on different forms. His published works include a study examining the importance of "unofficial" databases and racial differences in understanding levels of deadly force used by the police.

Ain A. Grooms, PhD, is an assistant professor in the Educational Leadership program at the University of Iowa. She studies educational opportunity with a specific focus on access and equity for Black students in K–12 contexts. She uses the intersection of race, place, and socioeconomic class to examine the impact of historical and contemporary educational policies—including school desegregation, school choice, and the retention of educators of color—on student achievement. Her research has been published in the *Peabody Journal of Education, Education and Urban Society*, the *Journal of Education for Students Placed at Risk*, and *Urban Education*.

Jennifer Maya Haan is currently a visiting assistant professor in the School of Teacher Preparation, Administration, and Leadership at New Mexico State University. The focus of her research is social justice leadership as related to the experiences of Asian American students in the K–12 public education system. Another research focus is addressing the ways in which educational leaders address racial equity in academic outcomes for Black, Indigenous, and people of color. She has served as a middle school teacher of English learners and an elementary special education inclusion teacher. She has also held various administrative positions in K–12 education in California, New Mexico, and Texas, including school site administrator and central office administrator.

Nicholas D. Hartlep is an associate professor of urban education and the chair of the Department of Early Childhood/Elementary Education in the School of Urban Education at Metropolitan State University in St. Paul, Minnesota. He also serves as the graduate program coordinator at the school. He has published 19 books, the most recent being *Asian/American Scholars of Education: 21st Century Pedagogies,*

Perspectives, and Experiences with coeditors Amardeep K. Kahlon and Daisy Ball (2018). In 2018, the Association of State Colleges and Universities granted him the John Saltmarsh Award for Emerging Leaders in Civic Engagement. Follow his work on Twitter at @nhartlep or at his website, https://nicholashartlep.com.

Samuel R. Hodge, PhD, is a professor of kinesiology in the Department of Human Sciences at The Ohio State University. He is a fellow of the National Academy of Kinesiology, the National Association of Kinesiology in Higher Education, and the Research Council of the Society of Health and Physical Educators of America.

Martha James-Hassan earned her undergraduate degree in kinesiology from the University of Wisconsin, Madison; her master's in inquiry education from Hamline University in St. Paul, Minnesota; and her doctorate in critical pedagogy from the University of St. Thomas in Minneapolis, Minnesota. She is a researcher, teacher, and leader with nearly 30 years of experience in urban education. She is currently an associate professor in the School of Education and Urban Studies at Morgan State University in Baltimore, Maryland. Her research agenda focuses on cultural fluency, interdisciplinary teaching, behavior management, and best practices in professional development.

Kenneth C. Land is the John Franklin Crowell Distinguished Professor Emeritus of Sociology and research professor in the Social Science Research Institute at Duke University. He is a fellow of the American Society of Criminology and the American Statistical Association. Known in criminology for his work on unemployment and crime rate fluctuations, structural covariates of crime rates, and finite mixture models of delinquent/criminal careers, he is the author or coauthor of more than 250 articles, chapters, and books.

Judson Laughter is associate professor of English education in the Department of Theory and Practice in Teacher Education at the University of Tennessee, Knoxville. He teaches courses in sociolinguistics, trends and issues in education, and critical teacher education. His research interests include critical race theory, culturally relevant education, and social justice education. He has published articles in *Review of Educational Research*, *Educational Researcher*, *Urban Education*, and *Teaching and Teacher Education*.

Chance W. Lewis, PhD, is the Carol Grotnes Belk Distinguished Professor of Urban Education at the University of North Carolina at Charlotte. Additionally, he is the founding executive director of the Urban Education Collaborative at the University of North Carolina at Charlotte, a premier center that focuses on producing groundbreaking research that highlights innovative teaching practices and solutions for urban schools, personnel, and communities at an international level. He can be reached at Chance.Lewis@uncc.edu; phone: 704-659-6842.

Roberto Lozano is a first-generation immigrant from the state of Chihuahua, Mexico. He serves as an associate superintendent for the Las Cruces Public School District but has served in different capacities within the public school system in the U.S.–Mexico borderland region. Additionally, he has worked as an adjunct instructor at New Mexico State University in the College of Education. His research interests and work are rooted in equity and educational access for underserved students in the pre-K–12 educational system, specifically Latino students and issues related to immigration and its implications to educational leadership.

Leanna Lucero holds a PhD in teaching, learning, and culture with an emphasis on mathematics, science, and technology education from the University of Texas at El Paso. She is an assistant professor and the director of elementary education in the School of Teacher Preparation, Administration, and Leadership at New Mexico State University. Her scholarship focuses on social justice complexities in teacher education with an emphasis on STEM disciplines and queer studies in education. She is dedicated to supporting populations that may not know how to access and navigate their rights in today's classroom, school systems, and world. She can be contacted at leannal@nmsu.edu.

Rick Marlatt is assistant professor of English language arts and literacy at New Mexico State University, where he received the College of

Education's Emerging Scholar Award in 2018 and was nominated for the Patricia Christmore Teaching Award in 2019. His work bridges the fields of teacher education, creative writing, digital literacies, literature study, and sociocultural theory. His recent interests include the cultivation of critical digital pedagogy in secondary English, incorporation of poetry writing into preservice teacher education, and the implementation of video games and virtual reality technology to enhance literature study and literacy identities for adolescents.

Melissa A. Martinez is associate professor in educational and community leadership at Texas State University. Her research focuses on equity and access issues along the P-20 education pipeline in relation to college access, readiness, and college-going cultures for underserved students; social justice, equity-oriented, and Latinx leadership/leaders; and the experiences of faculty of color. She is coeditor of *Latino Educational Leadership: Serving Latino Communities and Preparing Latinx Leaders Across the P-20 Pipeline*. Some of her work can also be found in *Leadership and Policy in Schools*, the *Journal of School Leadership*, and the *Journal of Research on Leadership Education*.

Patricia L. McCall is Professor Emerita of Sociology at North Carolina State University. Her research is embedded in the study of crime and social control, including ecological analyses of homicide and suicide, identifying the social and economic factors that explain the variations in these phenomena across geographic locations and over time—most recently studying European homicide. Other areas of research include latent trajectory analyses, modeling criminal careers, country-, city-, and macro-place-level homicide trends, juvenile justice program effectiveness, and projections of juvenile violent crime rates.

Chris Milk-Bonilla, PhD, specializes in building community and teacher leadership around bilingual and Latinx education. He received his degree in cultural studies in education from the Department of Curriculum and Instruction at the University of Texas at Austin. He currently teaches preservice elementary teachers ESL instruction. He has published articles on bilingual teacher and community leadership development around critical issues in Latinx education. He has led workshops on how to integrate the community into educational programs, improving home–school relationships, and community educational leadership development. He combines his knowledge of community organizing and instructional theory and practice to promote more inclusive Latinx community-based educational leadership.

H. Richard Milner IV is the Cornelius Vanderbilt Chair of Education and professor of education at Vanderbilt University. He has secondary appointments as professor of sociology and professor of education policy studies at Vanderbilt. His research interests concern urban education, teacher education, African American literature, and the social context of education. His most recent books are *Start Where You Are but Don't Stay There* (2nd ed., 2020), *Rac(e)ing to Class* (2015), and *These Kids Are Out of Control* (2018). He can be reached at rich.milner@vanderbilt.edu.

Whitney Sherman Newcomb, professor and chair of the Department of Educational Leadership in the School of Education at Virginia Commonwealth University, teaches courses on social justice and equity in leadership and ethical leadership. She is the author of more than 50 published journal articles and book chapters and three books. Her research interests include leadership preparation and mentoring, women in leadership, social justice in leadership, and ethical leadership.

Angela V. E. Owens holds a bachelor's degree in interdisciplinary studies (early childhood through fourth grade), dual master's degrees as an instructional specialist in early childhood and educational administration, and a PhD in literacy/biliteracy from the University of Texas at El Paso. She works with early childhood and special education teacher candidates at New Mexico State University. Her research interests include caregiver experiences with the special education process, early childhood education, and inclusivity for all children. Her experiences range from teaching in K–12 and special education settings to serving as a professional development consultant, a liaison for families who have children with special needs, and an elementary campus administrator. She can be contacted at avowens@nmsu.edu.

Magdalena Pando is an assistant professor in the School of Teacher Preparation, Administration, and Leadership in the College of Education at New Mexico State University. She is on the faculty of the Bilingual and Teaching English to Speakers of Other Languages (TESOL) program. She conducts research with in-service pre-K–12 teachers who are seeking their bilingual and TESOL teaching endorsements to teach culturally and linguistically diverse students. She also carries out research in STEM and science education in K–12 instructional settings. Her research methods are informed by theories in culturally relevant education, second-language acquisition, sociolinguistics, systemic functional linguistics, and model-based inquiry.

Karen F. Parker is professor and chair in the Department of Sociology and Criminal Justice at the University of Delaware. Her current research interests include exploring the influence of macro-level constructs on urban violence, particularly labor markets, racial segregation, and concentrated disadvantage. Much of her recent work has incorporated change models to examine how shifts in the local urban economy differentially influence race-specific homicide rates, including racial differences in the crime drop. Research on these topics has been published recently in *Social Science Research*, the *American Journal of Public Health*, *Urban Affairs Review*, and *Justice Quarterly*.

Chadrhyn Pedraza serves as an adjunct professor in the College of Education at New Mexico State University, where she received her PhD. Her areas of interests and research are in ethno-racial identity construction with a particular focus on Asian Americans and Pacific Islanders, the grounded theory method, educational leadership, and culture. She received her BA in psychology from the University of California, Los Angeles, and her MEd from the Harvard Graduate School of Education. She is a military spouse who has worked with military families for more than 14 years and currently resides in Germany.

April L. Peters, PhD, is associate department chair and associate professor in the Department of Educational Leadership and Policy Studies at the University of Houston. Additionally, she has practitioner experience in the K–12 context as a teacher and as dean of students, social worker, and principal. Her research interests include examining the ways in which districts mentor and support early career administrators, the intersectional identities for Black women leaders, and leadership and urban small-school reform. She is published in the *Journal of School Leadership, Teachers College Record*, the *International Journal of Qualitative Studies in Education*, and *Urban Education*.

Rosa L. Rivera-McCutchen is an associate professor and coordinator of school building and district leader graduate programs at Lehman College, City University of New York, a Hispanic-serving institution in Bronx, New York. Her research examines critical caring and effective urban school leadership and the impact of community and school contexts on reform efforts. Her research has appeared in *Urban Education*, the *Journal of School Leadership*, and the *Journal of Cases in Educational Leadership*, among others. She served as the AERA Division A 2017 program cochair and 2018 program chair and is the current chair of the AERA Leadership for Social Justice Special Interest Group.

Cristóbal Rodríguez, PhD, is an associate professor of educational leadership and policy studies and director of graduate studies in the School of Education at Howard University, where "the goal is the elimination of inequities related to race, color, social, economic and political circumstances." His research focuses on diverse demographics and explores how policy and leadership influence equity and access for diverse populations throughout the educational pipeline. In 2016, he was recognized with the White House Initiative on Educational Excellence for Hispanic Faculty Honors by the U.S. Department of Education program, recognizing scholars across disciplines.

Mariela A. Rodríguez, PhD, is a professor in the Department of Educational Leadership and Policy Studies at the University of Texas at San Antonio. She earned her PhD from New Mexico State University as a W. K. Kellogg fellow through the Hispanic Border Leadership Institute. Her research supports the educational attainment of Latinx English learners. Her work has been published in such venues as the *Journal of School Leadership* and the *Journal of Latinos and Education*. She is past president of the University Council for Educational

Administration. She is also a recipient of the Distinguished University Faculty Award from the Texas Association of Chicanos in Higher Education.

Brenda Rubio, PhD, is an assistant professor at New Mexico State University in the School of Teacher Preparation, Administration, and Leadership. She received her PhD in educational policy and planning and her MA in cultural studies in education at the University of Texas at Austin. Her research focuses on grassroots educational leadership, bilingual and dual-language teacher education, and culturally relevant education.

Monique Sloan, EdD, is the instructional supervisor of the Peer and Assistance and Review program for Prince George's County Public Schools. Prior to taking on this role, she served as the principal of Calverton Elementary located in Beltsville, Maryland. She was the principal of Calverton for eight years and truly loved working and inspiring her teachers toward greatness. In her current role, her hope is to help increase teacher support and retention by enhancing and expanding the Peer Assistance and Review program. She holds an EdD in educational leadership and policy studies from Howard University. Her areas of research focus on applied critical leadership, critical race theory, equity, leadership preparation, and advocacy for marginalized groups. She is a national conference presenter and hopes to continue sharing her experiences as principal and as a researcher with her colleagues throughout the world. Recently, she has published two articles focusing on principal leadership development and how to utilize the recommendations of the Kirwan Commission as a school leader. One of her greatest joys is seeing the teachers and building-level administrators grow and develop in their respective careers. She believes that teaching and learning is her life's work, and she hopes to continue growing and developing as a "lifelong learner."

Ursula Thomas, PhD, is the associate chair of cultural and behavioral science online and assistant professor of education at Perimeter College at Georgia State University. Her research interests include diversity, social justice, culturally relevant pedagogy, cultural mediation, multicultural education, gender issues in curriculum and teaching, service learning, STEM, technology, and leadership. She earned a BS degree in early childhood education from Alabama State University and received a master's degree in early childhood education from Auburn University of Montgomery. She earned an EdD at the University of Alabama in 2003.

Kristine Andrea Velásquez is a doctoral candidate in the Educational Leadership Doctoral Program at New Mexico State University. She was born in the border city of El Paso, Texas, and earned her BS and MBA degrees at the University of Texas at El Paso. Her dissertation topic consists of studying the ascension of university Latina administrators in the Southwest. Her research interest includes utilizing qualitative phenomenological approaches in understanding social justice leadership issues in higher education. The theoretical frameworks that interest her the most are feminist theory and critical race theory along with their branches.

Alexander Vigo-Valentín serves as a public health adviser in the Division of Policy and Data at the Office of Minority Health. Previously, he held an associate faculty position in the College of Health Professions at Towson University. His research agenda includes health promotion behaviors and school-based health policies affecting physical activity and obesity, especially among youth from disadvantaged and vulnerable communities. He received his doctoral degree in physical education teacher preparation at The Ohio State University.

Sarah W. Walters is a doctoral student in the Department of Educational Leadership and Policy Analysis at the University of Missouri. Inspired by her years teaching in urban schools, her research interests are in education policies, specifically those that impact issues of segregation and diversity.

Terri Watson is an associate professor in the Department of Leadership and Human Development at the City College of New York. Her research examines effective school leadership and is aimed to improve the educational outcomes and life chances of historically excluded and underserved students and families. Her scholarship is featured in several edited books and journals, including *Educational Administration Quarterly*, the *Journal of Cases in Educational Leadership*, the *Journal of Negro Education*, and *Leadership and Policy in Schools*.

Anjalé D. Welton, PhD, is an associate professor in the Department of Education Policy, Organization, and Leadership at the University of Illinois at Urbana-Champaign. Her research examines how shifting sociopolitical contexts influence how school leaders address issues of equity, especially race. Other research areas include college and workforce readiness and access, especially for students of color, and the role of student and community voice in school improvement and policymaking.

John A. Williams III, PhD, is an assistant professor of multicultural education in the Department of Teaching, Learning, and Culture at the College of Education and Human Development at Texas A&M University at College Station. His research focuses on developing and replicating best practices, policies, and personnel to dismantle inequitable discipline outcomes for African American students in K–12 school environments. Additionally, his research investigates how to prepare and support culturally inclusive teachers through the adaptation of multiculturalist frameworks. He can be reached at jwilliams3@tamu.edu; phone: 217-979-3453.

www.ingramcontent.com/pod-product-compliance
Lightning Source LLC
Chambersburg PA
CBHW051813230426
43672CB00012B/2716